"A charming story of perseverance and family bonds. Young readers will root for Jack to succeed as he faces increasing obstacles."

—*Kirkus Reviews*

"*Marvelous Jackson* is an unputdownable book, full of spirit, heart, and tons of Wisconsin charm—just like Jackson and the wonderful people that surround and support him. If you need a story full of hope, determination, second chances—not to mention cookies, cakes, and nuggies—look no further! This is your book."

—Sarah Miller, creator and author of the "Can We Read?" newsletter

"*Marvelous Jackson* is a purposeful page-turner kids can't put down! Like the best books, *Marvelous Jackson* takes you to places you want to be and introduces you to characters you want to befriend. It's familiar and fantastical; emotional and empowering. And most of all, it keeps you wanting more."

—Christina Lorey, journalist and UpNorthNewsWI.com editor

"Laura Bird's sweet, inspiring story shows the importance of showing up for others and the value of strong relationships. This exceptional book has the best recipe for making life's every moment count."

—Liz Swanson, elementary school instructional coach

"I loved this book! These characters reminded me of my friends. I'd recommend this book to anyone!"

—Nora Butler, age 11, voracious reader and daughter of acclaimed Wisconsin author Nickolas Butler

"Bird's descriptive writing once again eloquently captures life in the Northwoods through vivid imagery and memorable characters. Jackson's journey is one middle grade readers will easily connect with as they find their way, too."

—Angela Maki, Northwoods native and school librarian

"Brimming with heart and peppered with Wisconsinisms, *Marvelous Jackson* shows us the power of kindness, friendship, and persistence. Hand this sweet story to all the middle-grade readers in your life."

—Megan Nigh, teen services librarian

"With a compelling voice and fully fleshed-out characters, Bird delivers a poignant tale that strikes at the heart with rawness and honesty. A stunner."

—The Prairies Book Review

"A moving and uplifting read that celebrates the strength of the human spirit and the transformative power of love, community, and self-discovery; a must-have purchase for all middle grade collections."

—BookView Review

"*Marvelous Jackson* captured me right from the start and carried me to the end with happy tears. I found myself cheering Jack on the entire way as he tackled each recipe and gained more confidence. This book is rich, layered with flavor and oh so tender, just like the best dessert should be."

—Annemarie Maitri, owner, Bloom Bake Shop

Marvelous Jackson

Laura Anne Bird

orangehatpublishing.com - Waukesha, WI

Marvelous Jackson
Copyright © 2024 Laura Anne Bird
ISBN HC: 9781645387664
ISBN PB: 9781645386919
ISBN EBook: 9781645386964
First Edition

Marvelous Jackson
by Laura Anne Bird

All Rights Reserved. Written permission must be secured from the publisher to use or reproduce any part of this book, except for brief quotations in critical reviews or articles.

For information, please contact:

www.orangehatpublishing.com
Waukesha, WI

Illustrator: Jayden Ellsworth
Cover & Interior Designer: Kaeley Dunteman
Editor: Lauren Blue

This book is a work of fiction. Names, characters, places, and incidents are the product of the author's imagination or are used fictitiously. Characters in this book have no relation to anyone bearing the same name and are not based on anyone known or unknown to the author. Any resemblance to actual businesses or companies, events, locales, or persons, living or dead, is coincidental.

For Annie and William, again

Winter = baking season. It's on.

—Taylor Swift

You learn things and you burn things.

—Chris Bianco

*I have discovered in life that there are ways
of getting almost anywhere you want to go,
if you really want to go.*

—Langston Hughes

One
Oops, Sorry

Just like the day before—and the day before that—Jackson Jefferson Wilson wondered how much trouble he could get away with at school. It was a little game he liked to play, because then he could feel like a winner at *something*.

As he walked to English class, he knocked the books from the arms of a sixth grader. "Oops, sorry," he called out.

He flicked water from the bubbler at everyone who was in line to get a drink. "Oops, sorry," he said.

He smooshed his face against the window of the science lab and blew, puffing his cheeks out like a warped hamster. On the other side of the glass, the teacher yanked down the shade, and Jack laughed. "Oops, sorry."

The hallway began to empty as students ducked into their classrooms, and Jack knew he would be late.

Miss Kibble will make her usual sad face when I walk in, but that's about it, he thought. *And it doesn't matter if my report card has a tardy on it. Or fifty of them.*

Ever since Jack's mom died—four hundred and seventy-two days ago, according to the running tally in his head—he hadn't cared about things like report cards or tardies. And it's not like Norm was paying attention, either. He was lost in his own head, no doubt obsessing over cheeseburgers.

With just a few seconds to go until the bell rang, Jack rounded the corner of the language arts hallway and rammed directly into a stocky, solid figure blocking his path. He flinched and jumped back when he saw who it was. Of all the kids at Evergreen, why did it have to be *Benny*?

"What the heck?" Benny yelled, shooting spittle all over his hockey jersey. "What're you trying to do, knock me over?"

Jack raked his hand through his tangled mop of brown hair. "You were standing in a stupid spot if you didn't want to be knocked over."

"Or maybe *you* were just being a klutz." Benny shoved Jack, which made Jack's backpack slide off his shoulder and thud to the floor.

How Jack wanted to punch the smirk right off Benny's pale, blotchy face! His hands automatically curled into fists, but before he could take a swing, there was a loud sniffle. Jack peered past Benny.

Marvelous Jackson

Pressed against his open locker, Theo Porter lifted his chin. It seemed as if he was trying to put on a brave face, except Jack noticed that his brown cheeks were wet.

The bell rang, and Jack felt its shrill echo all the way down in his toes.

"What're you doing to Theo?" he hollered at Benny.

"I'm not doing anything."

"I don't believe you! Leave him alone. He's just a fifth grader, and he's half your size. Don't be a jerk!"

Benny cackled. "Takes one to know one." Sharp and fast, he kicked Jack in the shin.

Jack lost his balance and crumpled to the ground, landing right next to his backpack.

Theo gasped.

Benny swiveled to leave, but there was no way Jack was going to let him walk away looking so smug. He grabbed Benny's ankle and yanked as hard as he could. "Oops, sorry."

Benny hit the floor like a conifer cut down at Christmas. Immediately he began howling, "My toof! My toof!" He rolled onto his back, and a red river gushed from his mouth.

Oh, no, Jack thought. He and Benny had fought many times before, but no literal blood had ever been spilled. "I didn't mean to hurt you, I swear," he said, but Benny didn't appear to be listening.

With a look of horror, Theo bent down and scooped up a gory little clump. "Oh my gosh, his tooth got knocked out."

Jack groaned. He'd managed to get away with a lot of things since seventh grade started, but something told him this time was different.

Jellybean, what in the world are you doing?

The words came from deep inside his head, but the voice sounded just like his mom's. He hadn't heard it in so long.

Instantly, he was ashamed that she had returned to him in a moment of pure humiliation. He'd never done mean things or hurt people when she was alive. He'd fallen so low, she wouldn't even recognize him.

Sluggishly, Benny climbed to his feet and clamped a hand across his lips.

"Wait! Don't forget this!" Theo handed Benny the tooth.

"Get a life, Wilson," Benny mumbled from behind his fingers. He staggered away, in the direction of the school office.

Jack stared at the ceiling, trying to swallow the bile and regret that had filled his mouth.

Theo stood over him and held out a small hand. "Do you need help?" he asked.

Jack ignored Theo's hand. "What was Benny doing to you?"

"He was bugging me about my project for Science Club."

"He's not even *in* Science Club. Why would he care what you're doing?"

Marvelous Jackson

"I'm researching squid and crayfish, and I got an awesome jar of preserved specimens as a birthday present. Benny has to do an experiment for biology class, and I guess he was trying to rip off my idea." Theo shrugged, as if he knew his ideas were great and therefore worth stealing. "Why'd you stick up for me, anyway? You didn't have to do that."

"Yes, I did." Jack closed his eyes and remembered how Theo, Lola, and Clare had rescued him the summer before—even after he'd bothered them mercilessly for more than two months.

Lola was Theo's big sister, and Jack was sure she still despised him for all the rude things he'd said to them. Clare was their best friend from Chicago, and by accident, Jack had shot her little dog with a BB gun. As if that wasn't bad enough, he'd gone and clunked his head on his dad's fishing boat and plunged into Lake Lyons. He would've sunk to the very bottom if Theo, Lola, and Clare hadn't teamed up to pull him out like a pitiful, rubbery noodle.

"You saved my life," Jack reminded Theo.

"Fair enough," Theo replied and held out his hand once more.

This time, Jack took it, but he made a point to draw up his own body weight. He didn't need Theo toppling over, too. "Benny's right. I *am* a jerk."

Theo pushed his thick tortoiseshell glasses up the bridge of his nose. His chestnut eyes looked enormous as he blinked.

Deep down, Jack hoped that Theo would disagree with what Benny had said, but Theo only blinked again.

Jack had to face the truth. Since his mom died, he'd turned into someone he didn't understand or even *like*. Sure, his downfall had started during the saddest time of his life, but he'd let it go on too long. He could see how far he'd strayed from the kid his mom had loved so much.

He struggled to catch his breath. It felt like he was drowning in the lake all over again.

"Jackson Jefferson Wilson!" Principal Engel bellowed from the other end of the hallway. It sounded like he was in a very bad mood. "Stirring up trouble once again, I see!"

"I didn't stir up anything," Jack said. "Benny started it."

"Benny may have started it, but you took it too far."

"But—"

"I've already called your father. He'll be joining us as soon as he can get here. We'll meet in my office."

"I just want to go to English class," Jack whined. He realized, for the first time, how *sick* he was of going to Principal Engel's office. He'd been there so many times, he knew the location of every pencil and potted plant.

"And *I* just want Benny's tooth back in his mouth where it belongs." A vein throbbed visibly across Principal Engel's forehead.

"Well, so do I!" Jack reached out and smacked the nearby row of lockers in frustration. The sting on his palm was instant. It felt like he'd been burned.

Marvelous Jackson

"Oh, no!" Theo exclaimed. "My experiment—"

His jar of preserved sea creatures trembled on the top shelf of his open locker.

Then it shifted.

And it fell.

Jack lunged, trying to catch the jar, but it slipped through his fingers as if it were smothered in bacon grease. It shattered, sending stinky formaldehyde, dead critters, and shards of glass rolling across Jack's tennis shoes. He glanced at Theo's pinched face. "I'm so sorry. I didn't mean to do that."

"It's fine," Theo said, but Jack knew he was just trying to be nice. "I can figure out something else for Science Club."

"But it was your birthday present . . ." Jack choked back his shame and nausea.

"You're going to have to clean up that mess, young man," Principal Engel said, shaking his head at Jack. "We'll get you some paper towels and a broom, and then we'll sit down with your dad and have a nice long talk."

Jack wiped his nose with the back of his hand as Theo gave him a look of unmistakable pity. He wished desperately to hear from his mom again—*You've got this, Jellybean!*—but no encouragement was offered.

I'm on my own, he thought.

It was time to face the music.

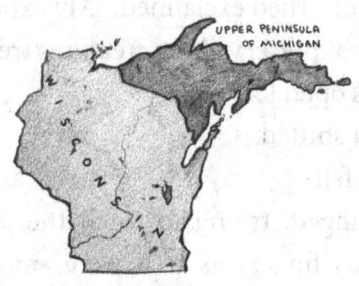

Two
No, Sir

"Suspended again." Principal Engel glared down his sledding hill of a nose at Jack. "For the second time since school started, and it's only November."

Next to Jack, Norm rubbed a hand across his face.

"I didn't mean to knock out Benny's tooth or break Theo's jar. None of that stuff will happen again . . . sir." Jack had never called the principal "sir" before, but now seemed like the right time to start. "I was just trying to stand up for Theo, but things went wrong."

"As you know, Evergreen has a strict no-tolerance policy for physical aggression," Principal Engel said.

Jack wanted to sink into the upholstery of his stiff-backed chair.

"It's a real shame that this altercation is on top of the *other* poor choices you've made at school this year,"

Marvelous Jackson

Principal Engel went on. "Being tardy to class, rolling your eyes at teachers, shooting spitballs all over the ceiling of the boys' bathroom—"

"And don't forget your first suspension," Norm added. "That whole fire alarm business."

"You're running out of chances, Jackson," Principal Engel said.

"What do you mean . . . sir?"

"What I mean is that a third suspension will get you expelled from Evergreen."

"What?" Jack's vertebrae snapped to attention.

"If you mess up again, you'll have to find a different school. Evergreen is unable to enroll any students who've been suspended three or more times," Principal Engel explained.

Norm looked alarmed. "You can't be serious."

"The policy is listed in our parent handbook, if you'd taken the time to read it at the beginning of the school year, Norman."

Jack was positive Norm had read *nothing* from Evergreen.

"But there are no other schools in Alwyn!" Norm shouted.

"I'm sorry, but I don't make the rules," Principal Engel said. "I believe Boulder Bay Academy would be the closest."

"But Boulder Bay Academy is more than thirty miles away! Jack can't go to school there!" The pouches under

Norm's red-rimmed eyes looked even puffier in the harsh glare of the fluorescent lights. "Look, I'm a single dad, and I'm just trying to run my restaurant. It's not easy doing all this without Jillian."

At the mention of his mom, Jack was reminded that Norm was grieving, too. *Maybe I'm not the only one who's a mess*, he thought. He put his hand on Norm's forearm and squeezed. He couldn't remember the last time they'd touched.

Norm patted Jack's hand distractedly. "I can't spend all that time driving across the Northwoods every day," he said through clenched teeth. "I'm sorry."

"It's not even a guarantee that Boulder Bay Academy would enroll Jackson to begin with." Principal Engel tented his fingers in front of his face. "They don't like to see multiple suspensions on a student's transcript, so perhaps a better option would be the Davy Crockett Institute of Outdoor Learning."

"What's *that*?" Jack asked.

"It's in the Upper Peninsula of Michigan—"

"The U.P.?" Jack exclaimed.

"It's a boarding school, so you would live there, Jackson, which means no long daily drives for you, Norman. The school teaches kids how to build log cabins, forage for edible mushrooms, go canoeing—"

"But I don't like to do any of that stuff!" Jack shrieked. As it was, he already felt like he didn't belong in his small, rural town. It seemed like everybody his age loved to hunt, fish, and hike—except him. The U.P. would be even more horrible. He'd *never* survive being forced to live like a pioneer.

"If you can improve your behavior, then you won't get suspended again and Davy Crockett wouldn't need to be a consideration at all," Principal Engel said.

"You can't get yourself kicked out of Evergreen. You gotta turn over a new leaf," Norm implored Jack.

Jack nodded. He knew Norm was right.

"Then I think we're finished." Principal Engel closed the folder that was open in front of him. "Your suspension starts now, and you can return to school the day after tomorrow. You're a good kid, Jackson. You've just gotten yourself caught up in some unfortunate circumstances. I know you can do better."

Principal Engel shook Jack's hand, and they all rose from their seats.

"How're things going at Dutch's?" Principal Engel asked Norm as they walked out of his office.

Jack appreciated the change of subject. It meant that he and his mistakes were no longer in the blinding spotlight.

"It's always crazy for us during deer hunting season," Norm replied. "We're packed every day for lunch and supper."

"And I bet all your patrons are dressed in their camouflage and blaze orange!" Principal Engel chuckled, and Norm joined in. "Are you planning to enter the first-ever Northwoods nuggie competition next month?"

"Darn tootin'," Norm said. "If Dutch's wins, there's a cash prize, recognition, and lots of publicity." He reached into the pocket of his jacket and pulled out a small, crinkly package. "I don't have any nuggies on me right now, but do you want to try one of these?"

Principal Engel sniffed the air as if he were a puppy. "Whaddya got there?"

"My latest batch of venison jerky." Norm handed him a stick.

Principal Engel sunk his teeth into the meat and chewed. "Oh, that's real good."

Norm looked pleased. "I threw some teriyaki in there, and Worcestershire, and loads of garlic. Do you get a hint of jalapeño as well?"

"I sure do." Principal Engel took another bite. "It's got more kick than a high-strung donkey."

Do not roll your eyes, Jack reminded himself.

"Want one?" Norm held out the package to him.

"No, thanks. You know I don't like venison," Jack said.

Principal Engel's eyes bugged out. "How can a kid raised in northern Wisconsin not like venison?"

A number of retorts blew through Jack's mind like a hot summer tornado, but he clamped his mouth shut before he could utter any of them out loud.

From this moment on, there was no room for error.

Three
It Hasn't Made an Ounce of Difference

Jack followed Norm out of Evergreen into the overcast afternoon. He turned toward the bike rack, but Norm hissed, "Where do you think you're going?"

"Um, to get my bike? You know—to ride home?"

"Nope. I'll drive you instead."

"Why?" Jack asked. He loved zipping around the country roads all on his own.

"You just got suspended for the second time, or do I have to remind you?"

"No, you don't have to remind me," Jack huffed. He put his bike in the bed of the pickup and climbed inside the cab.

"We need to have a little chat," Norm said, giving his car keys a fierce jingle.

Jack shuddered. He knew that a *little chat* was inevitable, but he didn't have to be excited about it. Why couldn't he just have a simple ride with his dad, with no confrontations or conflict?

Norm started the ignition, and Jack stared out the window at the trees lining the road. Their branches were stark against the gloomy sky, and he wanted to rip them out of the ground and throw them like spears. *But I've got bad aim, so they wouldn't get very far.*

"It's not just at school where you need to improve your behavior," Norm said. "You have to clean up your act at home, too. It's like you've hit rock bottom everywhere."

Jack didn't need Norm to clarify. In the last month alone, he'd gotten caught playing ding-dong ditch, breaking the windows of an old woodshed on someone else's property, and "borrowing" Rebecca Danner's bike without asking—for an entire Saturday.

"If you can't stay out of trouble while I'm at the restaurant, then you'll have to join me there after school and on the weekends. There are *tons* of things you could do for me, Dusty, and Rusty."

"But I don't want to work at Dutch's!" Jack screeched. He loved Dusty and Rusty, but he didn't want to smell like Buffalo sauce and onion rings every day. Plus, he'd spent his entire life listening to his dad yammer on and on about recipes and ingredients. He liked leaving some space between himself and Norm's intensity.

Marvelous Jackson

"Then you can sit in a booth and do your homework instead. I'll be able to keep an eye on you that way," Norm said.

Jack pictured all his independence drying up, just like the prunes his grandparents ate down in Florida. "But I'm not a toddler. I don't need a babysitter."

"Oh, really?" There were deep grooves along Norm's forehead as he frowned at Jack.

Jack sighed. "OK, fine. Maybe I needed a babysitter *before*, but I won't need one starting right now."

"Oh, really?" Norm asked again. "How do you figure?"

"I promise to stay out of trouble."

"But how're you going to do that, exactly? You have way too much free time on your hands, and that's when you make bad decisions."

"What if I . . ." Jack wracked his brain for anything that could save him. "What if I find a hobby? Then you wouldn't have to watch me like I'm a little kid."

"You're going to find a *hobby*?" Norm lifted one of his eyebrows, which was as fuzzy as a caterpillar.

"Yep."

"What will it be?" Norm pressed. "And don't even think of saying 'playing *Candy Smash*,' because you've been doing that all along, and it hasn't made an ounce of difference."

"Um, well." Jack pushed his shaggy bangs off his face. "I guess I need to think about it for a little while."

Norm grunted. "Don't think about it *too* long. I need to know what your plan is going to be, or you'll be hanging out at Dutch's, effective immediately."

I can't mess up at school, and I can't mess up at home. Jack swallowed thickly, longing for the way his life used to be. He'd never had problems like this when his mom was alive.

I miss her, he thought. *And I miss my dad, which is weird because he's sitting right next to me.*

Suddenly, and with an urgency that made his eyes sting, Jack wanted to get back to being the person he was before.

Because he realized how much he missed him, too.

Four
Candy Smash

The next morning, Jack began his suspension day with good intentions. He turned on some music—pulsing and shrieky with aggressive guitars and mind-numbing drums—and sat at the kitchen table. Over breakfast, he would figure out what his new hobby would be.

He shoveled a spoonful of Bountiful Berry Biscuits into his mouth.

"Drawing?" he said out loud. "Chess?"

No. Neither of those things felt right.

"Volunteering?"

Sometimes he had helped his mom at the library by shelving books and setting up displays, but there was no way he'd *ever* go back there without her.

"Electric guitar?"

As much as he loved the wailing of heavy metal, he'd never played an instrument before. He wasn't even sure he could read all the musical notes.

"Yoga?"

He tried to imagine balancing on one foot while holding his arms out like tree branches. It made him laugh so hard, he accidentally snorted the milk he'd poured on his cereal.

"Computer programming?"

He liked video games, but not enough to actually *make* them.

Jack slurped down the rest of his Bountiful Berry Biscuits and went into the living room, where he slumped in front of the television. He was sure that playing *Candy Smash* for a couple minutes would help him come up with some better ideas.

But hours later, when his phone buzzed and jolted him back to reality, the only thing Jack had come up with was a new way to infiltrate Cocoa Castle.

Norm

Have you stayed out of trouble today?

Jack

Norm

Did you decide on a hobby?

Marvelous Jackson

Jack

Norm

Why not?

Jack

Working on it

Jack frowned at the television. *Candy Smash* had done nothing for him but waste time. He turned it off as fast as he could. He needed to focus.

Norm

Get cracking! Want me to bring you carryout for supper later?

Jack started to reply with a thumbs-up emoji but quickly deleted it. Even though he hadn't come up with a hobby yet, he wanted to show Norm—and himself—that he was serious about making a fresh start.

I'll ride my bike to Dutch's for supper, he thought. *Which is NOT the same thing as being held prisoner there.*

He didn't mind going to the restaurant on his own terms. Plus, he could offer to taste test Norm's nuggies. He knew Norm would love that idea.

Jack: How about I head over to Dutch's

Norm: Sure! Saves me a trip to the cottage, but I thought you didn't want me to babysit you here . . .

Jack: You're not babysitting me . . . I'm choosing to be there, and I can try some of your nuggies, too

Norm: Great. Come before the dinner rush.

As long as venison wasn't involved, Jack would eat anything. Including nuggies—although he wasn't exactly sure what they were.

Guess it's time to find out.

Marvelous Jackson

...

To get to Dutch's, Jack had to bike up and down rolling hills, through the woods, and around Lake Alwyn and Lake Lyons. He also had to pass right by Evergreen, where Carlos and Pogo were playing football in the field.

"Hey, *niño!*" Carlos yelled across the yellowing grass.

For the thousandth time, Jack wondered why Carlos had nicknamed him "kid." It made no sense, because they were the same age and had known each other forever. Plus, Jack was taller than Carlos *and* Pogo. Didn't his height count for something?

He pedaled toward them.

"Did you really trip Benny and knock out his tooth?" Pogo called out.

Jack didn't answer. He hated that the news had already spread through school.

"But why'd *you* get in all the trouble? Benny always starts stuff and then gets away with it. He needs to stop being such a jerk." Carlos whipped the football at Jack, but Jack couldn't dive for it since he was still on his bike. The football bounced off his tire and spun to the ground.

Jack shrugged. "Maybe I need to stop being a jerk, too."

Carlos and Pogo stared at him before dissolving into laughter.

"What? You don't think I can do it?" Jack sputtered.

They shrugged.

"Thanks for the vote of confidence." Jack dropped his bike and helmet in the grass and swooped down for the football. After so many months of feeling numb, he suddenly wanted to prove his friends wrong.

"You're lucky you missed social studies, dude. We had a sub, and he was horrible," Pogo said as he flicked his blond hair. "What'd you do all day?"

"Just gamed," Jack said.

"*Candy Smash* again?" Carlos sighed. "Will you be too busy tracking down evil lollipops and dodging butterscotch discs to hunt with me and Pogodinski sometime this week?"

Both Carlos and Pogo knew he wasn't a hunter—of deer, turkeys, or any animal with legs or wings. "Like you guys would even want me to go out with you! I'd shoot one of you in the foot by accident or fall out of the deer stand," Jack said.

"It's sooo hard being awkward and uncoordinated," Carlos cooed.

Jack tried to give him a noogie, but Carlos dodged it.

Jack's phone buzzed.

Norm

Nuggies are almost ready

Jack

👍

Marvelous Jackson

Norm

Hurry!

Jack slid the phone into his back pocket just as the football—which he hadn't been paying attention to—smacked against his forehead.

"Sorry, dude! You OK?" Pogo yelled.

"I'm fine, but I gotta go eat supper at Dutch's." Jack rubbed his skull and found that a lump was already forming. "I need to show Norm that I'm making a change."

"Is he mad at you for getting suspended again?" Pogo asked.

"Yep." Jack climbed back on his bike. He pictured the disappointment scribbled across Norm's face in Principal Engel's office, and he vowed never to see it again. *No more trouble at school. No more trouble at home.*

"Good luck, *niño*," Carlos said.

"Thanks," Jack replied as he pedaled away, but he knew his fresh start had nothing to do with luck.

It was all on him to make things better.

Five
Test Test

When he got to Dutch's, Jack put his bike and helmet behind the restaurant and pushed open the rickety screen door, which went right into the kitchen. Inside, the air felt muggy and compressed, just like August. He peeled off his hoodie, and there was a clatter of pans that reminded him of Bacillus Maximus, his favorite band.

"Jackal!" Rusty hollered. "How ya doin'?" He was stirring a pot of noodles while flinging wedges of sweet potato into the deep fryer. Under his white chef coat, his studded leather necklace gleamed against a black t-shirt with a skull and crossbones on it. "Ope! What happened to your forehead? Looks like you got yourself a big ole lump."

"It was just a run-in with a football. I'm fine."

Marvelous Jackson

"If you say so." Rusty drained the pasta, and for a minute Jack couldn't see his face through the curls of steam. "Your dad's around here somewhere. Dusty's working front of house, and I'm on cooking duty. I heard you want to try our nuggies."

Jack nodded.

Rusty pointed at a stool with a pair of tongs. "Sit."

Jack obeyed, and his stomach growled like a far-off motorcycle.

Rusty tossed him a blaze orange apron. "Put that on."

The apron was so fluorescent, it made Jack's eyes hurt. On the front, it said *WE ♥ SERVING HUNGRY HUNTERS.* He sighed and tied it around his neck.

There was a flurry of movement while Rusty fried and scooped. His ruddy, round face broke out in a grin as he set a platter in front of Jack. "Your evening meal, sir," he said, bowing.

"Thanks," Jack said, and reached for a nuggie.

"Not so fast." Rusty threw a roll of paper towels at him. "Good manners are valued at this fine dining establishment."

Jack ripped off a square and dropped it next to his plate.

Rusty brandished his tongs again. "Where does that belong?"

Jack put the paper towel in his lap and studied the three sizzling brown lumps on the platter. They didn't look like chicken fingers or chicken tenders. They didn't look like chicken nuggets, either. They were fatter and wider, and Jack couldn't think of a better word to describe them than *nuggies*.

"We've got three versions of our fine fowl for you to try, Jackal, and we're excited to hear what your discerning palate thinks."

"I have a discerning palate?" Jack said, amused.

"Sure thing. You've got good taste buds, just like your old man."

Jack shrugged. He'd never thought about his taste buds before, but he seriously doubted that he and Norm had anything in common.

As if on cue, Norm pushed through the swinging door between the dining room and the kitchen, with Dusty following close behind.

Beyond them, Jack could see the "laid-back, up-north charm" that Dutch's was known for, which meant dead animals looking down from the walls, trophy fish strung along the rafters, and a vintage *Sonic Boom* video game machine that usually ate people's quarters.

"Jacky!" Dusty almost ruffled Jack's hair but wrinkled his nose and gave him a fist bump instead. "Young man, do you know the meaning of the word 'comb'?"

"Yes, I know the meaning of the word 'comb.'" Jack eyed Dusty's plaid flannel shirt and perfectly groomed beard. "At least I don't look like a fancy lumberjack."

Marvelous Jackson

"That's exactly the vibe I was going for." Dusty swatted Jack with a dish towel.

Norm sat on the stool next to Jack's. "Speaking of wardrobe—Rusty, button that chef coat of yours all the way to the top!"

"Sure thing," Rusty said. His skull and crossbones disappeared behind the stiff white material. "Sorry, boss."

Norm turned to Jack. "How's your supper?"

"I don't know. I haven't actually eaten anything yet—because of all the talk about manners, hair, and fashion." Jack pretended to glare at Rusty and Dusty, but they just laughed.

"We gotta choose one of these three nuggie recipes to use for the competition, so I sure do appreciate your help," Norm said.

See? I'm putting my best foot forward, Jack thought while shoving a nuggie into his mouth.

Norm watched Jack closely as he chewed. "Well? You like it?"

Jack nodded. "It's good."

"We bathed that one in an egg mixture, dredged it through flour and spices, and fried it in peanut oil."

Jack took another bite. He didn't care what had been done to the chicken. It was hot, savory, and satisfying, and he told Norm as much.

"Why don't you try the second one?" Norm pushed the platter closer to Jack. "We marinated it in milk and butter, rolled it in breadcrumbs and Parmesan cheese, and then threw it in the oven. I'm just not sure the spices are *wow* enough."

Jack bit into the nuggie. "The Parmesan has a nice kick, but I think the chicken needs more salt. It's not bad, but I like the first one better."

Norm rubbed his hands together. "Now we're getting somewhere."

Jack chomped into the third nuggie. "This one is definitely my favorite."

"Why?"

Jack considered his dad's question. "Well, I like how it crunches between my teeth. There's a burst of spice and salt—but not too much. The color of the nuggie is nice, too. Sort of orange-y, which makes it look special. You could say there's a wow factor."

Rusty pumped his fist. "See, Jackal? I *knew* you had a discerning palate."

I can't believe I just used the phrase "wow factor," Jack thought.

"We brined that one in buttermilk, hot sauce, and vinegar, and then we fried it in canola oil. We still need to fine-tune all the spices for the batter, but I think that's the recipe we should use for the competition," Norm declared.

"Absofrickinglutely," Rusty belted out. He waved a wooden spoon at Jack. "Now, don't you go tellin' anybody about our ingredients, Jackal. If I find out that you've given away our secrets, I'll break both your legs."

Jack laughed.

"Just kidding. I'd never break your legs. Maybe an arm or finger, but that's it."

Dusty stroked his dark beard. "All joking aside, fellas, the first-ever nuggie competition isn't going to be a walk in the park. More than twenty-five restaurants have entered, which is way more than anybody expected. They're from all over the Northwoods—Hazelhurst, Eagle River, Park Falls, you name it. Dutch's needs to be at the *top*. We've got our exceptional reputation to uphold."

"And the winner gets a five-thousand-dollar prize," Norm said. "Think about what we could do with all that money! We could replace the carpeting, or get the walls repainted, or buy a bigger salad bar."

"Or update our deep fryers," Dusty said.

"Or maybe get a few new video games, like *Master Blaster* or *Martian Attack*," Rusty said.

"Or *Rapunzel Rescue*," Jack added.

"We gotta win the competition first," Norm said. "Back to work, boys."

Rusty returned to the stove, and Dusty departed for the dining room.

"You're sure you don't want to work here?" Norm asked Jack.

"I'm sure."

"At the very least, you could take up cooking for your hobby! You've got a knack for talking about food and ingredients, buddy."

Jack squirmed on his stool. "I guess I just want to find something that's my own."

Norm narrowed his eyes. "You don't want to cook at Dutch's, and you refuse to do any activity that requires fishing rods, hunting rifles, or sporting equipment. What does that leave?"

Jack wasn't sure, but he had no plans to give up so quickly. That was something the old Jack would've done.

"Don't worry," he told Norm. "I'm going to figure it out."

Six
Fungi

With his suspension behind him, Jack returned to school the next day.

He didn't shoot one spitball. He didn't flood any toilets with wadded-up toilet paper. And he wasn't late to English class.

When he passed by Principal Engel in the cafeteria at lunchtime, he gave a polite nod. He felt Principal Engel's eyes on him as he kept walking, and he held his head a little higher. *I will not give that guy the satisfaction of seeing me get booted out of Evergreen.*

When the bell rang that afternoon, Carlos caught up with him in the hallway. "Football?"

Jack shrugged.

"You got something else going on?"

"Math homework, and maybe—"

"No more *Candy Smash*! You gotta get a life, *niño*!" Carlos said.

Those words again: *Get a life*. Benny had told him the exact same thing after their fight.

Jack sighed. He couldn't deny that he was getting sick of *Candy Smash*. He'd played it so much, his backside had permanently smooshed the rug where he always sat. "Fine. Let's play football."

"That's the spirit! Meet me and Pogo in a few minutes." Carlos hurried off, and Jack took a step toward his locker—but as he did, something hard and heavy came smashing down on his heel. His tennis shoe flipped off as he pitched forward. At the last second, he threw out his hands to keep his face from smacking into the floor. "What the . . . ?"

Benny stood above him, smirking. "Wanna fight?"

Yep, Jack thought. It felt like his heart was going to gallop right out of his body, but he forced himself to shake his head. He wasn't going to blow his last chance at Evergreen on Benny. "No, I do not want to fight." He shoved his shoe back on and stood up.

"You sure?"

"I'm sure."

"That's too bad." Benny grinned, and Jack recoiled. The knocked-out tooth was back in its spot!

Benny smiled wider. "You like what my dentist did?"

Jack couldn't answer. He wondered if this whole thing was a joke.

Marvelous Jackson

"It hurts like crazy, but at least I get to eat ice cream for the next month. Soft food only."

"How'd your dentist *do* that?" Jack managed to ask.

"She stuck the tooth back in the socket and attached it to the teeth that are next to it. See?" Benny pulled back his lips and got right in Jack's face.

Jack didn't relish being so close to Benny's mouth, but he peered inside anyway. "That little wire is connecting them?"

"Yep, and hopefully the root will reattach."

Jack felt like he might throw up. This was the most he and Benny had ever talked, and here they were, discussing revolting teeth stuff.

"This whole thing's gonna cost my parents *five hundred dollars*," Benny announced.

Jack cringed.

"And I'm sure they'll be sending you the bill."

Jack let the air out of his mouth—slowly, slowly—because he had to stay calm, no matter what. "I understand why your parents might want me to pay for your tooth, but you started the whole thing when you picked on Theo and then kicked me in the shin."

"But *you* grabbed my ankle, which made me fall on my face."

"Well, two minutes ago, *you* stepped on my heel and almost made *me* fall on my face," Jack countered.

Benny moved an inch toward Jack.

For a fleeting second, Jack thought Benny was going to deck him with one of his baseball-mitt-sized hands. He took a step back, so he was just out of reach. *No more fighting*.

"Fair enough," Benny muttered, and he took off down the hallway.

Jack stared at Benny's retreating figure and wondered how he would ever come up with five hundred dollars.

There was a tap on his shoulder. He whirled around, fully expecting another confrontation.

"Hello," Theo said.

"Oh, hi," Jack said.

"Are you all right?"

"Why wouldn't I be?"

"I saw you . . . trip."

"You saw me *get* tripped."

"Well, are you OK?" Theo asked.

"I'm fine."

Theo nodded sympathetically.

Jack knew there was something important he needed to do while Theo was standing there in front of him. "Hey, I'm sorry again about breaking your jar and killing your ocean critters."

Theo shrugged. "Don't feel *too* bad. They were already dead."

"Right." Jack shifted from one foot to the other. "But I apologize for losing my temper and doing something dumb without thinking."

Marvelous Jackson

"Apology accepted. If it makes you feel better, I've decided to change my science project anyway. I'm going to study tree bark and fungi, which means my scientific samples won't be stored in preservative liquid. If they break, there won't be any formaldehyde or glass splinters."

"Oh," Jack said. "Nice."

"I was wondering if you wanted to come over to my house."

"Me?" Jack looked over his shoulder, but nobody else was around. "Why?"

"Why not? We can hang out and talk about tree bark. My mom will make us a good snack."

The only houses Jack had been invited to for as long as he could remember were Carlos's and Pogo's. He'd forgotten how to spend time with other people, and he doubted that tree bark and snacks would be enough to pass the time with a fifth grader adopted from Ethiopia that he barely knew. But he felt like he owed Theo. He couldn't say no.

"OK," he agreed.

"How about tomorrow after school? Do you want a ride? One of my moms always picks me and Lola up. She can drive you, too."

"Thanks, but I'll just bike over."

Theo's sister wouldn't want me in their car, anyway, Jack thought. Since summer, Lola had understandably kept her distance from him.

Theo gave Jack his address, but Jack already knew exactly where his cottage was, on the far west side of Lake Lyons. Alwyn was so small that everyone knew these things. When the Porters' moving van had rolled in from Milwaukee the year before, the whole town had paid attention, even if they'd pretended not to.

"I guess I'll see you tomorrow, then," Jack said.

"It'll be great! I can't wait to show you my desiccated sulfur shelf and comb tooth."

Jack tilted his head. He had no idea what Theo was talking about.

"Fungi," Theo said as he waved goodbye. "Funnngggiii!"

Jack didn't understand how somebody could find toadstools so fascinating, but his lips twitched into a smile. Maybe Theo could teach him something.

Seven
Charcuterie Board

The next afternoon, Jack stood on the steps of Theo's cottage and stared at the bright red door, which was decorated with a wreath of twisted autumn branches and dried berries. He ran his hand through his hair as he pictured the dirty doormat and pot of dead geraniums that graced his own front steps.

Suddenly, Jack was nervous about going inside. He couldn't understand why Theo would want him around. He gazed longingly at his bike, which he'd propped against the Porters' garage. He could ride home, turn on *Candy Smash*, and drown all his worries in the quest for Fudgie Chews.

No, you can't do that, he reminded himself. *You're changing your life, remember?*

Before he could chicken out, he knocked.

Theo whipped open the door so fast, Jack wondered if he'd been waiting on the other side the whole time.

"I thought you'd never get here," Theo said.

Jack swallowed. "I'm here."

Theo gestured for Jack to follow him inside.

Immediately, the smell of butter, cinnamon, and sugar hit Jack squarely in the face—harder than he'd ever been slugged by Benny.

"My mom's baking," Theo said, as if it weren't obvious.

"Whimsydiddles?"

"How'd you know?"

"My mom and I used to make them together." Jack pictured his mom in her flowered apron, and he grinned. After four hundred and seventy-five days, it felt good to remember her doing something she loved instead of wasting away in a hospital bed.

"Oh." Theo dipped his chin. "I'm sorry."

"It's OK, really. It's nice to talk about her," Jack said, and he meant it.

Theo led Jack into the kitchen. "Mom, this is Jack. Jack, this is Marisa, one of my moms."

Marisa was shorter than Jack, but the dark, floppy bun on top of her head made her seem taller. "It's so nice to meet you!" she exclaimed.

Jack didn't know what to do with his arms, his feet, or his face.

Marisa handed him a thick wooden board heaped with

Marvelous Jackson

food, and he took it from her without dropping anything, which was a win. "Make yourself at home," she said.

Jack sat at the kitchen table next to Theo, and he gaped at Marisa's platter. It was covered with strawberries, purple grapes, grainy crackers, cheese cubes, and chunks of dried meat, which he was relieved to learn were pork—not venison. He loved all the bright colors and textures in front of him. "You weren't lying about your mom giving us a good snack," he said to Theo.

"I go overboard every time I make a charcuterie board." Marisa added a handful of mixed nuts to the platter and frowned. "Please tell your dad I'm sorry for wrecking your appetite. You won't have any room left for dinner."

Charcuterie board, Jack repeated in his head. He was glad to know what it was called. "Don't worry about wrecking my appetite. That never happens," he said.

Norm had texted Jack to say he couldn't bring home carryout that night, so Marisa's snack would be his supper, anyway. *We're hosting the Mercer Lake Buck Boosters' annual dinner*, Norm had written. *We're expecting so many folks, we've got an ENTIRE GALLON of ranch dressing ready.*

Jack practically pounced on the charcuterie board, but Rusty's voice shouted at him from inside his head. *Put a napkin in your lap! Don't chew with your mouth open! Show off your nice manners!* He obeyed Imaginary Rusty.

As Jack and Theo ate, they talked about Theo's new science project, Lola's involvement in Drama Club, and the boxing gym that Theo's other mom, Abby, owned.

"How'd you guys come up with all your hobbies, anyway?" Jack asked.

Theo gave him a funny look. "Why do you want to know?"

Jack shrugged. Embarking on his search for a hobby had made him wonder about other people and how they chose to spend their time.

"I guess it's all about getting into a flow state," Theo replied.

"What's that?"

"It's when you're focused on what you're doing, and you're not distracted. You feel . . . uplifted and inspired."

Jack thought about *Candy Smash*. Did gaming uplift and inspire him?

The answer was easy.

No. It left him with sore thumbs and blurry eyesight.

When the only thing left on the charcuterie board was a tangle of bare grape stems and green strawberry leaves, Theo washed and dried the platter, and Jack put their dirty plates in the dishwasher.

"What do you want to do now?" Theo asked him. "We could hang out with Lola, who's practicing Shakespeare in her room. Or I could show you my new samples of birch polypore. Or we could go to the boxing gym and hit the bags for a while." He made two little fists and launched into a flurry of uppercuts.

Jack opened his mouth, but nothing came out. His brain ticked through all the things that he was sure would go wrong with each of Theo's suggestions.

Lola would kill me if I bothered her.

I'm not exactly interested in birch . . . whatever it's called.

And I've never hit a boxing bag before, so I'd probably do it all wrong—which means the bag would end up punching me instead.

But Jack knew that for someone who urgently needed a hobby, he was ruling things out left and right.

"Or we could just bake," Theo added.

"Oh." Jack's hands got a little sweaty. "Bake?"

Theo nodded.

"But . . . I haven't baked in a while, and I've only ever baked with my mom." Jack wondered if he could do it without her. What if he messed up? Even worse, what if he broke down in tears from missing her so much?

"It's OK," Theo said hurriedly. "We don't have to bake at all. We can do something else. I didn't mean to—"

"No, let's do it," Jack said, surprising himself.

Theo smiled. "It's like riding a bike. It'll come back to you right away."

Marisa tossed Jack a red apron.

He read the words written across the front in white. "Wauwatosa East?"

"It's where I went to high school, in Milwaukee. I worked concessions at all the basketball games, and that was the apron I wore." Marisa pushed a mixing bowl into his arms. "There are a dozen Whimsydiddles in the oven that need to come out in five minutes, and I just started measuring ingredients for a second batch."

Jack stared at the stainless-steel bowl, and he saw the reflection of his face. Maybe he had a discerning palate when it came to fried food at Dutch's, but it had been a long time since he'd helped his mom make something sweet.

"The recipe I'm using was passed down from my grandmother," Marisa said. "It's one hundred percent foolproof, so you can't mess anything up, even if you tried."

Before Jack could worry about making a mistake, Theo asked if he wanted to crack the eggs—and he did, because it was weirdly gratifying to split a creamy white shell into two neat cradles. Then he softened yellow pats of butter in the microwave while Theo combined flour, cinnamon, and cream of tartar.

After they'd stirred everything together, Jack rolled the cookie dough into balls and placed them on the baking sheet. Theo was right: it was like riding a bike. He didn't have his mom nearby, but his fingers and hands remembered just what to do.

Jack was so intent on giving each doughball enough space, he almost didn't notice when Lola sauntered into the kitchen.

Marvelous Jackson

When she saw Jack, she pursed her lips as if she'd just scarfed down a bag of Sour Mollycoddles.

"Oh, hi." Jack tried to sound relaxed, even as he panicked. He was standing in front of a girl who'd seen him at his very worst. His ball of dough missed the cookie sheet and fell to the floor with an audible splat.

Lola grabbed a banana from a bowl on the counter and swiped one of the cookies that Marisa had just taken out of the oven.

"They're not cool yet!" Theo told her.

"Yum," Lola said, despite the steam coming from her mouth. "Hope your next batch turns out as good." She pointed at the dough on the floor and laughed.

"Be quiet, Lola," Theo said.

"'Some are born great, some achieve greatness, and some have greatness thrust upon them,'" Lola announced in a crisp British accent as she left the kitchen. "But some, none of the above."

"Oh, be nice!" Marisa cried.

"*Twelfth Night* by William Shakespeare," Lola yelled from the hallway. "Act two. Scene five. In case you were wondering."

"We weren't!" Theo yelled back.

"Sorry for making a mess." Jack wiped the floor with a dishrag, but he only made the greasy spot worse.

"I'll take care of it." Marisa took the rag from his hand. "Your dough needs you."

Jack went back to organizing balls on the cookie sheet as he contemplated the Shakespeare line Lola had just recited. She'd meant it as an insult, of course, but he wondered if she was on to something.

For the first time in possibly forever, he decided that *he* wanted to be great, too.

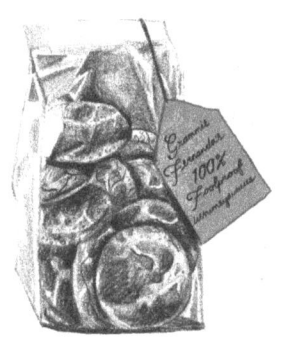

Eight
Obsessed

After they cleaned up the kitchen, Theo asked Jack if he wanted to stay a little longer. "We could watch a show," he said.

"What show?"

"*The Marvelous Midwest Kids Baking Championship!*" Theo exclaimed. "Have you ever seen it?"

Jack admitted he hadn't.

Marisa told Jack to sit, and she switched on a small television in the corner of the kitchen.

"*The Marvelous Midwest Kids Baking Championship* season starts with twelve contestants," she explained. "They're ten to thirteen years old, and Shane O'Shaughnessy, the host, gives them all kinds of crazy things to do. Each episode, one baker wins the challenge, and another one is sent home. At the end of the season, the last baker standing is awarded the grand prize of twenty thousand dollars."

Jack couldn't believe that a kid could win so much money for being on a baking show. He also couldn't believe how fast Marisa talked.

Theo cranked the volume on the television as the camera zoomed in on Shane O'Shaughnessy, whose dimples gleamed in the dazzling light.

"Welcome to *The Marvelous Midwest Kids Baking Championship*, filmed in the Windy City of Chicago, Illinois!" Shane O'Shaughnessy said. He opened his arms as if to embrace the entire world.

He turned to the contestants, who were standing in a row. "For today's challenge, each of you must bake something that incorporates at least three different kinds of candy."

"Yum. Candy," Theo said.

"You can make whatever you'd like—cookies, scones, muffins, you name it," Shane O'Shaughnessy went on. "And we have oodles of candy for you to choose from." He pushed a cart toward the contestants, and they oohed and aahed over the buckets of Caramel Dots, bowls of chocolate buttons, and trays of pink licorice.

"I'd use *all* that," Theo said.

"It's easy to go wild in a challenge like this, but restraint is everything, Theodore. Just because you *can* doesn't mean you *should*," Marisa said.

"Yes, Mother," Theo said, deadpan. He turned to Jack. "Sorry. We're a little extra when it comes to *MMKBC*."

Marvelous Jackson

"It's OK," Jack replied. Theo didn't understand that Jack had nowhere else to be, and that no one was waiting for him at home—which meant that listening to them discuss *The Marvelous Midwest Kids Baking Championship* wasn't a problem.

As soon as Shane O'Shaughnessy blew his golden whistle and bellowed, "Your time starts right now!" Jack couldn't tear his eyes away from the screen. His muscles twitched as the contestants tore through the sleek industrial kitchen, preheating ovens, grabbing pints of heavy cream, and creating a frenetic whir with their beaters, blenders, and mixers.

Midway through the episode, Jack finally spoke. "Do you think the contestants ever get nervous?"

"I'm sure they do at first, but they seem to get comfortable in front of the camera pretty fast," Theo answered.

"But how do they know what ingredients to use, and what recipes to make?"

"They can't use any cookbooks on the show, so I suppose they memorize basic recipes at home. Then they amp them up, depending on what they have to make for the challenge."

"That makes sense," Jack replied. A few minutes later, he pointed at one of the contestants. "What's her name again?"

"Ruby," Theo and Marisa answered at the same time.

Ruby had made a sheet cake, which she'd carved into chunks and sculpted together using frosting as glue. By the time she was done, she'd constructed an actual cake basket.

"I didn't know you could do that!" Jack cried.

"You can do almost anything on this show," Theo said.

Ruby chose Rainbow Lassoes, Fruity Whips, and Sugar Ribbons from Shane O'Shaughnessy's candy cart, and she braided them together to make a handle. Then she attached the handle and filled her cake basket with Glitter Balls.

"That's *incredible*," Jack said.

"Meanwhile, poor Otis is in big trouble," Marisa said.

"But I love Otis," Theo wailed.

Jack asked who Otis was.

"He's the one who tried to bake a candy pie," Marisa said.

Jack nodded. The heat from Otis's crust had melted the Fudgie Chews he'd stuffed inside, which led to a brown, oozy mess.

"The clock is ticking, bakers!" Shane O'Shaughnessy announced, and there was a surge of noise in the kitchen. A minute later, he began his official countdown. When he got to zero, he blew his golden whistle and yelled, "Time's up!"

"Now the bakers have to present their treats to the judges for their critiques," Theo said.

Marvelous Jackson

Jack scooted his chair closer to the television. He imagined the warmth of the *MMKBC* kitchen, the floury feeling of the contestants' hands, and the sense of accomplishment that came from making something from scratch.

The first judge—a woman who was as long and thin as a pair of kitchen shears—scrutinized every item through a magnifying glass before taking a single dainty bite. She explained to one contestant that his muffin wasn't sweet enough. She told another that her donut was too dry.

"Does anyone ever get anything *right* on this show?" Jack wondered out loud. He watched the contestants for signs of anger or frustration, but they all appeared to calmly listen to the judges' feedback—even Otis, with his disgusting pie.

"Of course, but there's usually room for improvement," Theo answered.

The second judge—a man who was as round as a morning bun—inhaled at least three bites of each item and looked like he would've eaten even more, if the lady judge hadn't given him the side-eye. He didn't use a magnifying glass, but he grilled each contestant about flavor, texture, and consistency. He asked one baker why she'd used almond extract instead of vanilla in her scone. He asked another why he'd skimped on the butter in his croissant.

Jack remembered what Norm always said: *Ingredients really do matter.*

After a commercial break, Shane O'Shaughnessy was back in front of the camera, smoothing his shiny hair and adjusting his pink satin pocket square. "Our judges have deliberated, and they've arrived at their decision. Today's winner of *The Marvelous Midwest Kids Baking Championship* is . . ."

"Insert dramatic pause here," Theo murmured.

"Ruby!" Shane O'Shaughnessy said.

Before he could stop himself, Jack applauded. It felt so good to let loose.

"But we have one baker whose treat just didn't cut it," Shane O'Shaughnessy continued. "The contestant we have to say goodbye to is . . ."

"Insert dramatic pause here," Theo murmured again.

"Otis."

Theo made a pouty face.

"I'm sorry, Otis. You've been burned. Put away your rolling pin because you're going home," Shane O'Shaughnessy said.

"But he's my favorite," Theo whined.

There was a giggle, and Jack turned to see Lola in the doorway. He wondered how long she'd been standing there, watching them watch the show.

"At least Roscoe didn't get booted off. He's *my* favorite." She flipped her long black braid in Jack's direction.

Jack couldn't tell if it was a friendly flip or not—but

at least she was talking to him, which was a start. "Which one's Roscoe? It's hard to keep everybody straight."

"He's from South Korea, like Lola. He made the candy pizza," Theo said.

"Oh, yeah. That was pretty epic," Jack replied.

"Do you see why I love this show so much?" Theo asked him.

Lola smirked. "Before you know it, you'll be obsessed, too."

"I guess there are worse things," Jack said.

He would've stayed at the Porters' house all night, but he figured they'd be eating supper soon, and he didn't want to get in their way. He stood up. "I should probably head out now."

"You might want to take off that apron first," Lola said.

"Oh, yeah." Jack gave an embarrassed laugh. "That would be an interesting look for riding across town."

Lola flipped her braid once more and left the kitchen.

Jack gave the apron back to Marisa. "Thanks for having me over. I had a great time."

"Why don't you let me drive you home, Jack? We can shove your bike in my back seat, or, better yet, Abby will be done with work soon, and she can take you in her pickup."

"It's OK," Jack said. "I know all the roads, and I've got a light mounted on my handlebars."

"Promise you'll be careful?"

Marisa's attention felt like a toasty fire in a drafty house.

"I promise," Jack said.

"Here, take these with you." She handed Jack a baggie that was filled with the cookies they'd made. She'd attached a recipe card written out in loopy cursive: *Grammie Fernanda's 100% Foolproof Whimsydiddles*.

"Thanks," Jack breathed. He slid the cookies in the outer pocket of his backpack, where they wouldn't get wrecked by his laptop and binder.

"Want to come over again sometime?" Theo asked.

"Yep," Jack said, and he wasn't lying.

"I think your mom would be proud of you for baking," Theo whispered.

Jack thought so, too. "Thanks," he whispered back.

After saying their goodbyes, Jack walked out the Porters' front door and was instantly swallowed up by cool autumn air. He waved at Theo and Marisa, who were framed by their living room window, and he felt their eyes on him as he got on his bike and rode down the driveway. At the end of the street, he turned to wave one last time, but they'd already closed the curtains. Above his head, a flock of geese honked, flying southward.

As Jack pedaled home, the sky settled into inky purple darkness, and the first stars of night emerged.

They reminded him of the sugar crystals he and Theo had used in their Whimsydiddles.

He skidded to a halt.

"Duh!" he yelled.

He tapped his knuckles against his head, as if to clear out all the cobwebs that had collected. He couldn't believe he hadn't thought of it sooner—but then again, he hadn't thought about *anything* important since his mom had passed away.

He felt as buoyant as helium, because the answer was right in front of him.

Baking can be my hobby!

Nine
Not a Prank

As Jack let himself into the dark, quiet cottage, his phone buzzed.

Unknown

Hi. Is this Jack?

He didn't recognize the number.

Unknown

This is Clare Burch.

"This must be a prank," Jack said out loud.
There was no reason why Clare would be texting him. He'd made a fool out of himself in front of her and even put her in danger.

Marvelous Jackson

Jack

> If you're looking for Jackson Jefferson Wilson, I can pass on a message to him, this is his personal secretary

Clare

> He has a personal secretary . . . ? Well, can you tell him hi from me? I was just texting with Theo. He said he and Jack had a great time baking together.

Jack groaned. He was an idiot. It really *was* Clare.

Jack

> JK, this is Jack, I don't have a personal secretary, you're gullible

On the other end: radio silence.

"I shouldn't have called her gullible!" he yelled.

After a full minute (Jack was counting), Clare texted back.

Clare

It's OK. It's true, I'm gullible sometimes

Jack

I didn't mean to hurt your feelings, how'd you get my number?

Clare

Theo gave it to me. I wish I wasn't so far away in Chicago, or I'd be hanging out with you guys, too. How'd your cookies turn out?

It occurred to Jack that he hadn't actually eaten any of the Whimsydiddles. He'd gotten so sucked into *The Marvelous Midwest Kids Baking Championship*, he'd forgotten all about them. He pulled out the bag from Marisa and popped one in his mouth.

Jack

Well they're cakey on the inside and crumbly on the outside, and they have a great balance of cinnamon and sugar

Marvelous Jackson

He laughed. He sounded just like Norm, except he was describing cookies instead of chicken.

Clare

My grandma and
I are gonna make
Peanut Butter
Buttons right now.
You've inspired me

Jack

Jack grinned. To his knowledge, he'd never inspired anyone before.

Clare

Gotta go preheat the oven now!

But Jack couldn't let her sign off yet. There was something important he needed to say.

Jack

BTW I'm really
sorry for acting
like a jerk over the
summer and doing
stupid stuff, I wish
I could go back and
change everything

Clare

I understand, thanks for the apology, Prez

Jack

Prez?

Clare

You have three very presidential names, don't you?

Jack

Ha, yes, my mom loved American history. With Wilson as our last name, she thought she and my dad should go all out with my first and middle

Clare

Jack

Have fun baking, City Girl

Clare

Thanks!

Marvelous Jackson

Jack grinned. It was incredible that Theo had given him a chance, and it seemed as if Lola might be considering it, too. But Clare? Her forgiveness was something he hadn't allowed himself to imagine.

This really is a fresh start, he thought, pledging not to botch it up.

Jack briefly wondered what recipe Clare and her grandmother were planning to use for their Peanut Butter Buttons, which made him jump up and begin rummaging through the kitchen cabinets. He found just what he was looking for.

Tenderly, Jack set the cookbook on the table. A few of the pages were dog-eared, and others were decorated with rings of olive oil and splotches of dried tomato sauce. He rubbed his fingers across the recipes as if they were a genie's lamp.

"Hi, Mom." He smiled, even though there was no response.

He flipped to the dessert chapter.

"Peanut Butter Buttons," he read out loud. "Chippie Chews. Snow Day Blossoms." It was like being reunited with old friends he'd forgotten about!

He wanted to make *all* the cookies, but his heart sank faster than the stones he'd tried (and failed) to skip in Lake Alwyn. The recipes were too hard for someone who'd never baked anything on his own before.

Jack pushed the hair out of his face. There had to be

something easier. He turned the page and was greeted with a photo of a puffy white cookie that had been his favorite when he was little.

Sugar Dumplings!

He could remember exactly how they tasted, and smelled, and felt on his tongue.

Slowly, Jack read the recipe, line by line. Unlike the others, it didn't seem too complicated.

He ran to the pantry, assuming he'd find all the ingredients he needed, but the only thing he unearthed was a measly bag of clumpy sugar.

Apparently, *zero* baking had occurred in the cottage since his mom had died.

"That's going to change, starting right now," Jack said.

He dialed Norm's number.

"Hi, buddy!" Norm said. In the background was the sound of running water and clanking plates. "The Mercer Lake Buck Boosters event is happening right now. We're swamped."

Jack had forgotten. "Oh, right. The gallon of ranch dressing and all that."

"Sorry I couldn't bring you carryout."

"It's OK. I ate a charcuterie board, and—"

There was a crash, and Norm swore under his breath. "What'd you say?"

"Nothing." Jack paced the kitchen. "Hey, could you leave out some money for me?"

"Money?"

Marvelous Jackson

"For the supermarket." Jack imagined Norm making a confused face at the phone. He'd never gone grocery shopping on his own before. "I need to buy some things."

"Sure. I'll leave cash on the kitchen table when I'm done with work, but it won't be until late."

Jack wasn't surprised. He was always asleep when Norm finished up at the restaurant. Norm would give a muffled knock on Jack's bedroom door to let him know he was home, and Jack would usually grunt in response—and that was the extent of their nighttime interactions.

There was another crash at Dutch's.

"That pan of pork schnitzel isn't done yet, Rusty!" Norm shouted.

"What do you mean? It looks done to me," Jack heard Rusty reply.

"Is it missing lemon slices?" Jack guessed.

"Yes, lemon slices!" Norm exclaimed. "How'd you know?"

Jack shrugged.

"You're *positive* you don't want to come cook with us? You've got what it takes, buddy."

"I'm good," Jack replied. "I just want to—"

There was a third crash, and the line went dead.

"I just want to make Sugar Dumplings."

Jack grinned and put his mom's cookbook back in the cabinet.

Ten
Hot Silver Frisbee

The wad of dollar bills Jack found on the kitchen table the next morning was greasy and smelled faintly of pork, but he grinned and shoved the money in his pocket. He would've thanked Norm personally, but his dad was snoring like a chainsaw upstairs in his bedroom. He scribbled a note of gratitude and left it on the counter for Norm to find later.

When school was done for the day, Jack rode his bike to the Alwyn supermarket and found all the ingredients for Sugar Dumplings. He had enough money left over to get a box of macaroni and cheese, a bag of baby carrots, and a pint of milk, too. He would make his own supper.

I'm staying out of trouble. I'm putting my best foot forward.

Marvelous Jackson

Jack paid for his groceries while the cashier nonchalantly sniffed the bills.

Yes, that's schnitzel, what's the problem? the old Jack would've sniped.

The new Jack just kept his mouth closed. He thought of something his mom had always told him: *If you can't say anything nice, don't say anything at all.* He wished he would've remembered it sooner. Maybe it would've helped him stay out of trouble.

Sorry, Mom, he thought.

Jack crammed the bags, boxes, and containers of food into his backpack and prayed that nothing would break during his ride home. The straps and seams shifted and groaned as he pedaled across town, and he found himself murmuring, "Stay strong. Don't give up." He couldn't bear to think about his eggs splattering on the street like little yellow bombs, or his flour trailing behind him like a dusting of snow.

But his backpack held, and he patted it in appreciation as he turned into his driveway.

...

A little while later, Jack was up to his forearms in dough while Bacillus Maximus thumped and crooned from the speaker.

He'd followed the directions in his mom's cookbook step by step—he was sure of it—but when he combined everything, the result didn't seem right. He put his nose into the mixing bowl and inhaled. It smelled good. He swiped a bite of the dough. It tasted good, too. But the texture was all wrong. He debated throwing it out and starting over, but he decided to keep going. He'd already come this far.

As Jack placed the doughballs on the cookie sheet, they reminded him of dense, miniature hockey pucks—not that he'd ever played hockey before. "They'd be perfect for Benny, that slug," he muttered. Benny played goalie for the Minocqua Muskies and never let anyone forget it.

He pushed the tray into the oven and wondered how long it would take for the Sugar Dumplings to turn golden brown.

But then he realized he hadn't set the kitchen timer.

"Nooo!" he yelled. When had he put the cookies in? Two minutes ago? Three? The recipe said the Sugar Dumplings needed to bake for at least eight. Now how would he know when they were finished?

He watched through the oven's glass door, and eventually, the Sugar Dumplings began to bubble around the edges, as if they each had their own pulse. Jack took that as a good sign. They *had* to be getting close.

But then he realized he'd forgotten to grease the cookie sheet.

"Nooo!" he yelled again.

In the middle of second-guessing himself about everything he'd just done, Jack's phone buzzed.

Marvelous Jackson

Theo

Want to watch MMKBC again?

Jack

Yes, my cottage?

Theo

Sure! Next week sometime?

Jack pictured the two of them hanging out at his place, and he grinned. His house had sat empty for too long. He couldn't remember the last time Carlos or Pogo had come over. He wanted to blame their absence on football or hunting, but he knew that he alone was responsible. He'd been so caught up in playing *Candy Smash* and getting in trouble, he hadn't thought to invite them. He was glad they hadn't given up on him.

Jack

His head whipped up from his phone.
Scorching!
The smoke detector began to bleat, which caused the neighbor's dogs to howl from their yard.
Jack opened the back door and frantically waved two potholders to clear the air. When that didn't work,

he pulled the scalding cookie sheet out of the oven and slapped it on the counter, all while the smoke detector and dogs kept up their insufferable racket.

The Sugar Dumplings looked just like lumps of charcoal. Jack tried to push them off the tray with a spatula, but they were unbudgeable.

His wail was almost as high-pitched as the smoke detector itself. This wasn't how his first solo baking project was supposed to go. His dad owned a restaurant, and his mom had been good at baking. He should be a natural!

In one sweeping motion, Jack hurled the tray across the kitchen. It sailed through the smoky air like a hot silver frisbee, smacking against the wall and clattering to the floor. Charred cookies rolled everywhere, reminding him of a gang of angry rodents.

Jack covered his face with his hands and moaned. He hadn't meant to lose his temper like that.

Finally, the smoke detector and dogs fell silent. All that remained was the screeching of Bacillus Maximus, which continued to blare through the cottage as if nothing had happened.

Jack uncovered his face and immediately saw the big black smudge he'd made on the wall.

Even worse, a large flake of paint had chipped off where the tray had smashed against it.

He grabbed a rag and began to scrub. Eventually the smudge vanished, but the chipped paint was a different story. He knew Norm would notice the blemish when he got home, and he'd want to know how it got there.

This is not a good way of showing him that I'm on a new path, Jack thought.

He ran to his bedroom and dug through the comic books, playing cards, old homework assignments, and ever-growing rubber band ball that littered his desk, until he found a bottle of Cover-It-Up. Back in the kitchen, he dabbed the correction fluid on the wall, blended it with the tip of his finger, and added a little more. It wasn't an exact match, but it would work.

Next, he washed the cookie sheet and swept the floor. He didn't stop until the kitchen was back to normal.

He pictured Otis from *The Marvelous Midwest Kids Baking Championship* and remembered how calm he'd stayed, even after messing up his candy pie. Unlike Otis, Jack hadn't gotten booted off a television show. He could simply try again.

He took a deep breath and made a new batch of dough. He rolled out the balls and was pleased when they didn't resemble pieces of sporting equipment.

He remembered to spray his tray and set the kitchen timer.

He pushed the cookies into the oven and pulled them out eight minutes later.

He sniffed them, poked them, and took a steaming-hot nibble.

"Yes!" he shouted, raising his hands in victory.

They were *exactly* how Sugar Dumplings were supposed to be: soft, unstuck, and proof that second chances sometimes paid off.

Eleven
As Long As You've Got Ingredients and an Oven

As his Sugar Dumplings cooled, Jack made the box of macaroni and cheese he'd bought at the supermarket. Afterward, he stared into the pot and lifted an eyebrow. The noodles looked so *basic*.

When he was little, he would've had a tantrum if someone—namely Norm—had sprinkled any seasoning on top of his food, but now he rooted around the pantry for jars of dried parsley and red pepper flakes. He tossed a pinch of each into the pot and admired the color and texture they gave the macaroni and cheese. He ate a spoonful and nodded happily. They gave the noodles a great flavor, too.

"It's always nice to have good spice," he said, quoting Norm.

Maybe he'd soaked up more of his dad's love of cooking than he'd realized.

Jack organized his Sugar Dumplings in small baggies and hid them behind a row of canned peaches in the pantry, where Norm would never find them.

It had been a long time since Jack had given a gift to somebody, and he didn't want to wreck the surprise.

...

The next morning, Jack got up earlier than he normally did on Saturdays, which is to say it was before noon. He wanted to catch Norm before he went to work, but according to a note he found on the kitchen counter, Norm had left the cottage at the crack of dawn. There was a broken garbage disposal at the restaurant, and he'd had to meet the plumber there.

In that case, I'll go to Dutch's myself, Jack decided.

He pulled three baggies of Sugar Dumplings from his secret stash in the pantry, tucked them in his backpack, and climbed on his bike.

"Hi, Jacky!" Dusty hollered when Jack walked into the kitchen. He was busy carving a glistening pink ham.

Rusty's eyes were just visible over a mountain of peeled potatoes. "What's up, Jackal?"

"Nothing. Is the garbage disposal fixed?"

They nodded.

Marvelous Jackson

"You here for food? Want a burger? Or maybe a cup of cheesy broccoli soup?" Rusty asked.

"Actually, I brought *you* guys something. Catch." Jack tossed them each a bag of cookies.

"What are these?" Dusty said.

"Sugar Dumplings. I made them."

"I didn't know you could bake." Rusty wiped scraps of potato off his hands.

"I didn't either. I mean, I used to make things with my mom, but that was a while ago. I'm not great at it yet, but I'm trying to figure it out."

Rusty ate one of the Sugar Dumplings. "Tasty."

Dusty put down his carving utensils and ate one, too. "Nice."

Norm glided in from the dining room. "Hey, isn't this the second time you've been here in the last couple days, buddy? For somebody who insisted that he didn't want to be babysat—"

"I know, I know," Jack interrupted. He knew Norm was kidding around, but he didn't want Dusty or Rusty to know about the consequences that were hanging over his head if he couldn't get his act together. "I just stopped by to bring you something, but it's not so bad hanging out here. It's kinda nice, actually."

"Awww," Norm, Dusty, and Rusty replied, in full-on teasing mode, but Jack could see a flush of sincere happiness spread across Norm's cheeks.

"Here, take these." Jack handed Norm a baggie of cookies.

Norm pushed an entire Sugar Dumpling in his mouth and chewed. "The vanilla really pops, and I like the undertones of brown sugar and almond. Didn't your mom used to bake something like these?"

"She sure did." Jack smiled. He loved that they were starting to talk about her so casually, remembering her as a person, not as a cancer patient. *It's taken us four hundred and seventy-seven days to get to this point, but at least we made it,* he thought. "I made this batch all on my own."

"Is that right?"

"Yep. I've found my new hobby."

"*Baking?*" Norm furrowed his brow.

"Yes, *baking.*"

"But . . ."

"But *what?*" Jack had hoped that Norm would be thrilled with his news. He hadn't anticipated any *buts.*

"Well, I guess a little part of me wished that you wanted to fry up walleye, just like your old man . . . but I think baking could be a real nice pastime."

"Yes, it could," Jack said.

Norm looked thoughtful. "I like that you're channeling your mom, and I like that you're spending time in the kitchen, but I have to be honest . . ."

"Honest about what?"

Marvelous Jackson

"Baking doesn't really strike me as a typical Northwoods hobby, especially for a boy." Norm frowned slightly.

Jack thought of *The Marvelous Midwest Kids Baking Championship* and how all the contestants were different. "You can't say stuff like that. Baking isn't a girl hobby, it's an *anybody* hobby. And it doesn't matter where you live, as long as you've got ingredients and an oven."

"He's right, boss," Dusty and Rusty said in unison from across the kitchen.

"OK, OK." Norm held up his palms.

"Even though I'm going to be busy with my new hobby, I promise to find some time to help out with your nuggies," Jack added. He knew that offering to lend a hand would go far with Norm. Maybe it would even help clear the slate of some of the thoughtless things he'd done in the past.

Norm's face shone, and Jack knew he'd nailed it.

"I'm glad to do more taste tests and even fine-tune your recipe if you want," Jack said.

"That'd be great," Norm replied.

"I could do some nuggie intel, too."

"Nuggie intel?" Norm's eyes grew big and dreamy.

Jack nodded. "And I'll help out at the competition next month."

"Thanks, buddy." Norm's cell phone rang, and he glanced at the screen. "Hey, I gotta answer this. It's my organic chicken farmer over in Sayner."

"Can I have more cash so I can go to the supermarket again?" Jack asked before Norm took the call.

He didn't know what he was going to bake next, but he was excited to start filling up his pantry. With the basics in place, he'd be ready for anything.

Twelve
Long Enough to Fit Thomas Jefferson

Jack spent most of Sunday reading his mom's cookbook, cover to cover.

He loved the big photographs of brownies and pies, and he practiced saying all the complicated words: *aerate, bloom, crimp, emulsify, temper.* They sounded cool, but he had no idea what any of them meant.

He wondered where he could find some easier recipes.

After school on Monday, he knew exactly where he needed to go—even if it meant getting razzed by Carlos and Pogo for bowing out of football.

He got on his bike, and a mile later, there it was:

ALWYN PUBLIC LIBRARY

Out of habit, he ignored the bike rack by the front

door of the building and instead went to the rear of the library, where all the employees parked. He left his bicycle in the woods next to the staff lot, which is what he'd always done when his mom was alive. He knew it would be safe among the pines and aspens.

As Jack emerged from the trees and walked toward the main entrance, a ripple of nerves made its way through his body. He wondered if he could handle being back at a place his mom had loved so much—but then he decided he was being silly.

You'll be fine, he told himself. *You might even have a nice time. After all, it's a place that you loved, too!*

Inside, the library was exactly how it had always been. The crinkling of newspapers, the quiet voices of patrons, and the warm, woody smell of books all seemed unchanged. The only thing missing was his mom.

But there she was, on the wall in front of him!

IN MEMORIAM
Jillian Wilson, Librarian.
For her years of selfless service and loving
dedication to the Alwyn Public Library.
She is deeply missed.

The words were engraved on a little metal plate, which was mounted on a smooth tablet of wood. Below the plate was a photo of Jack, his mom, and Norm, taken in happier

Marvelous Jackson

times. He peered closer at the photo and couldn't believe how much he'd grown since it was taken. He looked like a little shrimp! How was he the same person at all?

The plaque was so much prettier than the cold, gray headstone that had been erected in the cemetery. He liked knowing that every person who walked into the library would see his mom's face. They'd read her name, and they would know she'd been loved.

Jack guessed it was Miss Jean Ann who'd made the plaque. She had been his mom's best friend and had always done nice things like that.

His eyes flicked to the circulation desk, but it was unoccupied for the moment, so he walked into the stacks of books. As if his feet were in charge, they took him directly to the history and geography section. It was the longest he'd ever been away from it.

Without missing a beat, he found his favorite book from childhood: *The Illustrated & Entertaining Encyclopedia of U.S. Presidents* by C. J. Bertorello. After everything he'd been through, it felt strange that the encyclopedia was still in its same old spot, seemingly untouched and unbothered.

All these years later, he knew the entire book by heart, particularly the sections that featured his own name:

> ***JACKSON, Andrew.*** *#7. Served as president 1829 – 1837. "Old Hickory" had a terrible temper.*

Both his parents died by the time he was fourteen years old, and he struggled for the rest of his life with sadness and frustration. He fought in nearly one hundred duels, and in his spare time, he raced and bred horses.

***JEFFERSON, Thomas.** #3. Served as president 1801 – 1809. This Founding Father and co-author of the Declaration of Independence was referred to as "Long Tom." He was 6' 2 ½" tall, and sometimes he wore a bathrobe and slippers to meetings so people would think he was down-to-earth. His hobbies included playing violin, studying fossils, and keeping mockingbirds as pets.*

***WILSON, Woodrow.** #28. Served as president 1913 – 1921. "The Schoolmaster" was the only president to have earned a PhD. He fought for shorter workdays so workers wouldn't be exploited at their jobs. He loved to play golf and ride horses.*

His head swirling with images of horses, fossils, and mockingbirds, Jack sighed. He'd been named after three very uncommon men. They'd held the most important position in the country, but Jack knew they'd also made lots of mistakes along the way—mistakes that weren't mentioned in the kiddie encyclopedia.

Marvelous Jackson

Sometimes Jack felt proud of his name, but other times it made him cringe. Why was nothing as simple as it appeared on the surface?

Something brushed against his back, almost as weightless as a butterfly.

"Jackson Jefferson Wilson, is that *you*?"

Jack spun around.

"It *is* you. What a sight for sore eyes! And I mean that in a literal sense because I lost one of my contact lenses this morning and can hardly see straight." Miss Jean Ann covered her mouth and giggled.

Jack hadn't spent any time with Miss Jean Ann since she'd dropped off a tuna casserole for him and Norm more than a year ago. Her food had been the best of all the sympathy meals he'd eaten during that awful time. After that, she'd stopped by the cottage and called a few times, but Jack hadn't responded—not because he didn't like her, but because he'd felt as frozen and rutted as a dirt road in winter.

"Hi, Miss Jean Ann." Jack missed the feeling of her hand as soon as she removed it from his shoulder.

She shook her long, wavy strawberry blonde hair. "My goodness, you've grown so much."

Miss Jean Ann was right. Jack was nearly as tall as her. "I guess I'm turning into Long Tom." He wondered if she would catch the reference. She'd always loved history, too.

She laughed. "You're not *quite* six feet, two-and-a-half inches tall, but I bet you will be very soon, young man."

Jack grinned. She'd caught it.

Miss Jean Ann leaned in close, and he could smell her little puffs of minty breath. "I've missed you, and I'm very happy you've come back."

"I'm glad I've come back, too."

"Are you here for something special? Or maybe you've already found what you're looking for." She pointed to the encyclopedia he was still holding.

Jack pushed C. J. Bertorello's book back onto the shelf. "Actually, I need a cookbook, for someone who's just learning how to bake."

"Sure thing. We've got lots of cookbooks for beginners. Why don't we scooch down to our home economics and family cooking?" They scooched, and Miss Jean Ann pointed out a long row of cookbooks. "There should be some great ones here."

Jack pulled a few off the shelf and was happy to find that the recipes didn't look like rocket science. "I think these will work."

"I have to get back to the circulation desk, but come get me if you need anything else."

"Thanks for your help," Jack said. "And . . . thanks for the tuna casserole you brought us after Mom died, and thanks for being so nice today even though I haven't come to the library in ages."

Marvelous Jackson

"Of course." Miss Jean Ann's big brown eyes filled with tears. She gave a wet sniff and told him she'd see him on his way out.

Jack assembled a stack of cookbooks and sprawled on the carpet just like he did when he was a kid. He paged through them one by one and chose three to take home, because that was all that would fit in his backpack.

He waited in line at the circulation desk, but when it was finally his turn to check out, he couldn't find his library card. He searched his wallet, his pockets, and every crevice of his backpack. No luck. "I haven't used it in forever," he told Miss Jean Ann. He pictured the mess that was on his desk at home and figured his library card was pinned deep inside it. "I'm sure it's in my bedroom somewhere."

Miss Jean Ann assured him it wasn't a problem. She typed his name into her computer and pressed her face right up to the screen so she could see all his information, sighing again about her botched eyesight. She scanned the cookbooks and handed them to Jack. "Now don't wait so long to come back again." She waggled her finger at him, but her eyes crinkled up at the corners, so Jack knew she wasn't *really* mad.

He thanked her and promised to return soon. He waved goodbye as Miss Jean Ann greeted the next person in line.

Jack passed his mom's plaque in the lobby and had a sudden vision of his empty cottage, which waited for him like a dark yawn. He didn't feel ready to go home yet, so he turned and walked back into the stacks. He'd stay a little while longer—and maybe even read on the whistle chairs in the kids' section.

When he was younger, Jack had thought that the whistle chairs were the best invention ever. They were stuffed, upholstered, life-sized things that came in the shape of a gym teacher's whistle. He'd loved to rest his back against the hump and stretch out his legs along the flat part.

Jack chose a few random books from the shelves: a collection of poems by Langston Hughes, a study of volcanic rock in Iceland, and a guide to Italian sports cars.

He located the blue and orange whistle chairs behind a toy bin filled with foam blocks. The green whistle chair was wedged against the wall, and the yellow and red whistle chairs were right next to the ancient, long-legged card catalog. The card catalog hadn't been used in years, but its wide, flat surface was perfect for book displays. Jack had loved crawling underneath it when he was little.

He dumped his backpack on the ground and pulled off his hoodie, which he tossed on the foam blocks in the toy bin. Since no one else was in the children's section, he lined up all the whistle chairs under the card catalog and nodded approvingly. The couch he created was long enough to fit Thomas Jefferson himself.

Jack's phone buzzed.

Marvelous Jackson

Norm

Lake perch for supper?
I can bring you
carryout.

Jack

But if Norm brought him carryout, Jack would have to leave the library, and he wasn't ready to do that.

Jack

Actually, I'm not hungry

Norm

You sure?

Jack

I'm sure, but thanks

Jack got on his knees and crawled underneath the card catalog, accidentally banging his head on the wood. More proof that he had grown. He rubbed his skull as he sunk into the soft imitation leather.

Once he was settled in his cozy sofa of whistle chairs, he sighed contentedly and opened the collection of Langston Hughes poems. It looked interesting, but Jack didn't get very far before his mind began to wander.

He switched to the book about volcanic rock, but he couldn't focus on that one, either.

Maybe the book about sports cars would do the trick.

He tried to concentrate, but the words on the page grew fuzzier and fuzzier.

He wondered if he needed a pair of contact lenses, just like Miss Jean Ann.

Thirteen
Two Bobby Pins

Jack rolled over the next morning and groped around for his quilt, but it had slipped off his bed.

The grogginess of sleep began to fade.

Why am I wearing my tennis shoes? And why is there a book stuck to my cheek?

Jack's eyes flew open, and he was greeted by the wimpy light of an autumn sunrise trying to stretch through the windows.

The windows of the library!

He sat upright and smashed his head for the second time on the underside of the card catalog. He fell back onto the row of whistle chairs and fumbled for his phone.

It was seven o'clock.

There were no texts from Norm, but Jack figured he was pacing the cottage in a state of outrage at that very moment. "He'll kill me," Jack moaned. "And then he'll babysit me for the rest of my life."

He sat up again, carefully this time. There wasn't enough room under the card catalog to straighten his spine, so he hunched over and tried to make sense of what had happened.

I must've fallen asleep and didn't wake up when the library closed last night. I bet Miss Jean Ann didn't see me because of her missing contact lens, and my bike wasn't in the rack in front, where everyone would've noticed it. No one knew I was still here!

Jack groaned at his slip-up. He'd made an honest mistake, but based on his past behavior, no one would *ever* believe it was an accident. They would assume he'd trespassed on purpose, because the old Jack would've done something just like that.

He crawled out from beneath the card catalog and threw on his backpack. How could he get out of the library without setting off a burglar alarm or getting arrested?

He didn't have time to put away the books he'd been looking at, so he left them on a whistle chair and mentally apologized to the librarians that would have to clean up after him.

Jack ran to the lobby, where his mom smiled down at him from the wall. She looked so peaceful, which was the exact opposite of how he felt. "I've loved being back at the library," he said to her. "But I didn't mean to spend the night. It was a mistake, I swear."

With one glance at the big double doors, Jack knew there was no way he'd be exiting through them. They were chained up with a few elaborate-looking locks that he didn't want to mess around with. He turned and raced to the rear of the library, where the staff lounge was located. He remembered it had its own private door that went out to the employee parking lot.

Jack rattled the doorknob of the staff lounge, but it was locked. He clenched his jaw so hard, he imagined his teeth flying out of their sockets, just like Benny's had.

The junk drawer, he thought.

He scurried behind the circulation desk. When he was a kid, the junk drawer had been a treasure trove of small, shiny, infinitely practical objects that his mom and the other librarians had used all day long. He was glad to find that it was still crammed with paper clips, pens, stamps, stamp pads, bookmarks, Allen wrenches, fake tattoos of bookworms, stickers of wise old owls, and rolls of wintergreen mints.

But where was the key to the staff lounge?

There were zero keys amidst the clutter, but Jack found a few bobby pins, which could work in a pinch. He raced back to the staff lounge with two of them clutched in his fist. He needed to move fast, or he wouldn't have enough time to bike home, beg Norm for forgiveness, and change clothes for school.

The last time Jack had picked a lock was at Halloween. He and Pogo had broken into Pogo's little sister's desk to steal all the Fudgie Chews and Honey Fizzies from her stash of trick-or-treating candy. Mavis was still mad about it, even though she had a full set of braces and wasn't supposed to be eating any of that stuff.

Jack remembered what to do as he bent, inserted, and wiggled the bobby pins inside the keyhole. "Please! You *have* to work," he begged them.

Finally, the lock clicked open, and Jack exhaled.

He moved quickly through the staff lounge, toward the door that went out to the employee parking lot. He saw that it had a simple metal push bar. *Jackpot!*

He could go right out, and no one would know he'd been there.

Except for Norm, of course.

He'll never let me come back, Jack thought, and it made him want to cry.

"Thanks for the sleepover," he whispered to the library as he opened the door. "I had a really nice time, even though I wasn't supposed to be here."

Then he sprinted out into the frosty morning.

The hair on his bare arms stood on end, and the bolt clicked shut behind him.

Fourteen
Hoodie

Jack covered his ears. He was prepared for a hailstorm of shouting to begin as soon as he entered the cottage, but the only sound was Norm rumbling like a tractor upstairs in bed.

Jack couldn't believe it. *He's sleeping!*

Wait—he's sleeping?

He didn't understand.

Jack reached for the doorknob of his bedroom, and suddenly everything made sense. He must've shut his door before he'd left for school the day before, which meant it had been closed all along. And because Norm didn't go into his room when he got home from Dutch's, he never knew Jack was gone in the first place.

Falling asleep at the library had been an accident, but

Jack couldn't risk making any more mistakes like that. "You are so unbelievably lucky," he said to himself.

As he went to his dresser to grab clean clothes, he looked down at his t-shirt and realized that his hoodie was back at the library, on top of the foam blocks in the toy bin. He was amazed that he'd biked the whole way home without noticing.

Jack made it to Evergreen with just two minutes to spare, and the smile he gave Miss Kibble as he stumbled inside the school was genuine.

At the end of the day, Carlos and Pogo found him in the hallway.

"*Niño!* You wanna go hunting with me and Pogodinski?" Carlos said. He was wearing camouflage, head to toe.

"I'm good."

"But I've got a crossbow you can borrow, and all the gear you need."

"I do, too, dude." Pogo removed his blaze orange hat and shoved it over Jack's head.

The old Jack would've exploded. *I don't like hunting! I hate venison! You should know that by now!* he would've said. But he could see that his friends were simply trying to include him. They'd known each other since preschool, and although they didn't share a ton of interests, Carlos and Pogo had been exceedingly nice to him since his mom had died. He'd been so self-absorbed, he hadn't paid much attention until now.

Marvelous Jackson

"Thanks for asking. Maybe another time?" Jack whipped the blaze orange hat back at Pogo. "You guys go scout for deer. I gotta go track down my hoodie."

...

"Golly, you're a quick baker!" Miss Jean Ann exclaimed from her spot behind the circulation desk. "Do you need more cookbooks already?"

"Not yet. I was just wondering if someone turned in a hoodie," Jack said.

People forget things at the library all the time. Act natural, he told himself.

"It's blue," he went on. "I think maybe I left it here."

"Let me go check the lost and found. I've got both of my contact lenses in today, so I can actually see what's in front of me. I'll be back in a jiffy." Miss Jean Ann disappeared into the office behind the circulation desk and returned a moment later, waving Jack's hoodie like a flag. "Is this it?"

"Yep." He reached for the hoodie. "Thanks."

"Glad to help—although I could've sworn you were wearing it when you checked out your cookbooks yesterday."

Jack shrugged and shoved the hoodie in his backpack so he wouldn't have to make eye contact with her. He didn't want to give off any suspicious vibes. He liked Miss

Jean Ann too much to get on her bad side, although he doubted she had one in the first place.

"Do you need anything else? How about a ride home when my shift is over?" she asked him.

"I've got my bike."

"Tomorrow is the first day of December, and you're still riding your *bike*?" Miss Jean Ann shrieked. "Aren't you *freezing*?" She gave a dramatic shiver, even though she was wearing a thick green turtleneck, a wool skirt, and tall brown leather boots.

"Nope." Jack would never complain about riding his bike in December, because at least he still had his freedom and independence. If he waited for Norm to drive him around, he would never go *anywhere*.

Jack said goodbye and went outside. He pulled out his phone and laughed, because he could hardly see the screen through the plumes of his warm breath.

Now that he'd avoided disaster with both Norm and Miss Jean Ann, he could think about his hobby again.

He shot off a text. *Want to bake at my cottage tomorrow?*

Theo responded right away. *I thought you'd never ask. Yes!*

Fifteen

It Smells Like Happy People Are Inside It

Theo showed up at Jack's front door the next afternoon carrying two brown paper grocery sacks. Marisa beeped from the driveway, and Jack waved. He took one of the bags from Theo and exclaimed, "Holy cow, this is heavy! What's *in* here?"

"We stopped at the supermarket on our way over. My mom basically bought everything in the baking aisle."

"She didn't have to do that," Jack said, but it occurred to him that if she hadn't, he and Theo would've only had the most elementary ingredients on hand—the ones he'd bought with Norm's wad of cash. Next time he would have to plan better.

"As you know, she loves going overboard. And she just wants to help," Theo said.

Jack took Theo to the kitchen, which he'd cleaned and polished from top to bottom. He'd even put a fresh coat of Cover-It-Up on the chipped spot on the wall.

He turned on his favorite music, but he knew that Bacillus Maximus wasn't for everybody, so he kept the volume low. "Should we unpack everything?"

Theo nodded, and together they pulled food coloring, chocolate chips, coconut flakes, and sprinkles from the grocery bags.

"I didn't know sprinkles came in so many shapes and colors," Jack said, staring at the jars in amazement. He gave one a shake.

"If you want to get technical, their real names are Razzle Dazzles, Golden Chips, and Baby Beach Balls," Theo said. He stacked muffin cups, parchment paper, and decorating tips next to the sprinkles.

"That makes them sound so fancy."

"I've learned from watching *MMKBC* that if you give simple things sophisticated names, you sound way more professional, and then you impress the judges."

Jack laughed, but he guessed that Theo was right. "Speaking of *MMKBC*, do you want to watch another episode?"

"Yes, but let's bake first." Theo rubbed his hands together.

Jack opened one of the cookbooks he'd checked out from the library. "I found a recipe for us. Right here, on page twelve."

"Vanilla Blooms," Theo read. "Yum."

Jack ransacked the kitchen drawers until he found his mom's stash of flowered aprons. He and Theo would look like grannies wearing them, but he didn't mind. He figured his mom would be pleased they were being used again, after such a long break. Plus, when he tied the apron around his neck, he could pretend that it was her embrace.

Jack and Theo measured, poured, and mixed. They sprayed the baking sheets, set the kitchen timer, and waited patiently for the dough to turn into cookies.

When they pulled their first tray out of the oven, Jack had an idea. "Hey, let's put some Razzle Dazzles on top of them." He was itching to open one of the jars.

"But Razzle Dazzles aren't included in the recipe."

"Can't we be a little creative?"

"Sure, why not?" Theo replied, and he admired how pretty the cookies looked with the sprinkles covering them.

An hour later, when their Vanilla Blooms were cooling on the rack, Jack noticed he had flour in his hair and butter on his jeans, just like his mom always did when she baked. The cookies shimmered, and the cottage smelled amazing for the first time in ages. *It smells like there are happy people inside it again,* he thought.

He had no idea where the last hour had just gone. It was as if the rest of the world had drifted away on a cloud.

"Hey, Jack, you've been friends with Pogo and Carlos for a long time, right?" Theo asked.

"Yep. Since I was three."

"Have you guys ever baked together?"

Jack shook his head.

"Why not?"

"They like doing outdoor stuff. Sometimes I play football with them, and once in a while we'll hang out together while they try to shoot a deer. It's not perfect, but it works for us." Jack shrugged. Despite their differences, he felt lucky to have them as friends. "The only person I've ever baked with is my mom—and now you."

"What about your dad?"

"Norm?"

"Who's Norm?"

"My dad." Jack laughed. "No, we haven't baked together. He would rather make grilled cheese sandwiches and jalapeño poppers."

"You call your dad by his first name?"

"Not to his face, but yeah."

"Why?"

Jack blew all the air out of his mouth. "I guess I haven't felt very close to him since my mom died." It felt unexpectedly liberating to be so honest.

"Why not?"

"He works at his restaurant all the time, and I basically spent every waking moment of the last year playing *Candy*

Smash and doing dumb things. We've tried to cope, but I think we've kind of lost each other along the way."

Theo looked thoughtful. "I hope you two can get back together. I don't know what it's like to have a dad, so I'm a little jealous."

Jack had never considered that anyone might be envious of him.

Maybe everybody feels like they're missing something or someone important, he thought.

"I'm trying hard to make some big changes, and so far, I'm doing pretty good," Jack said. *Minus my accidental library sleepover.*

"Glad to hear it." Theo pushed his glasses up his nose. "Do you want to bake something else?"

"How about something with coconut?" Jack suggested.

Theo skimmed the cookbooks and found a recipe for Cocoroons while Jack stuck his nose into the bag of coconut flakes and took an extravagant whiff. "I forgot how much I love this stuff."

He and Theo measured, poured, and mixed, but when the instructions told them to beat their egg whites until they became stiff, they hesitated.

"I didn't know egg whites could get stiff," Jack said. "I thought they were gloppy and wet."

Theo tapped his chin. "Me too."

"How're we supposed to know what to do?"

"The internet, of course." Theo used his phone to do

some research. "It says here we need to use an electric mixer to beat our egg whites into soft peaks. Then we add sugar until the peaks stiffen."

The directions didn't seem complicated, but right in front of his eyes, Jack's egg whites turned into dry, stubborn clumps. He felt a familiar frustration rising inside him, until he recalled his ruined batch of Sugar Dumplings and how he'd totally overreacted.

Just start over. It doesn't have to be a big deal.

The second time around, Jack added the sugar to his egg whites gradually, without rushing, and sure enough, stiff peaks formed. They reminded him of tiny mountains, just like the instructions said they would. He and Theo high-fived each other.

When their Cocoroons were nestled in the oven, they went to the living room, and Jack was thankful that Theo didn't ask about the flat spot in the carpet. His *Candy Smash* addiction seemed like it had happened long ago, in a different life, and Jack was happy to leave it in the past where it belonged.

They threw themselves on the couch, and Jack turned on an *MMKBC* episode from an earlier season. This meant he struggled all over again to keep the names of the contestants straight, until he decided that it didn't matter who was who. He was more interested in what each contestant baked—like their cherry-bomb cupcakes, tie-dye layer cakes, and zucchini muffins.

"How do they do it?" he wondered aloud.

"Do what?"

"*Everything.* The contestants have to follow all the rules that Shane O'Shaughnessy gives them. They have to be creative without going overboard. They have to watch the clock so they don't run out of time. And *then*, when they're all sweaty and tired, they have to listen to Vicky Willow and Archie Gomez rip them to shreds."

"I think they practice hard, and learn from their mistakes, and have confidence in themselves. You know—basic stuff like that."

Jack laughed and threw a cushion at Theo's head. "Basic stuff that is sometimes very hard for someone like me."

Theo laughed and threw the cushion back. "I think you need to give yourself a little more credit."

Jack had never done that before. "Maybe you're right."

When the *MMKBC* episode was finished, Jack and Theo divided up the Vanilla Blooms and Cocoroons and organized them in baggies.

"Don't forget to take your leftover baking supplies with you," Jack reminded him.

"I'm leaving everything here. You'll use it, won't you?"

Jack nodded. He hoped Theo didn't notice the tears of gratitude nicking his eyes like little scalpels.

A horn tooted from the driveway. "I gotta go. My mom's outside," Theo said.

"Which one?"

"Abby. She just finished teaching a class at her boxing gym."

"Do you call them both Mom, or do you have different names for them?" Jack had been wondering about that, but he wasn't sure if it was OK to ask.

Theo didn't seem bothered by the question. "Both of them are Mom, which is only a problem when Lola's screaming 'Mooooom' super dramatically because she needs something, and they each come running at the same time." Theo rolled his eyes as he pulled on his mittens.

To Jack, that didn't sound like a problem at all.

But instead of pining for what Lola and Theo had, he smiled and patted the apron that was still tied to his chest.

After four hundred and eighty-one days, it felt like he'd gotten a little piece of his own mom back.

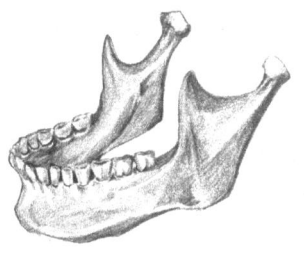

Sixteen

Jawbone

At school the next day, Jack found Carlos and Pogo in the hallway and handed each of them a baggie.

Carlos examined the Vanilla Blooms and Cocoroons. "What *are* these?"

"Um, cookies," Jack answered. "Isn't that obvious?"

Carlos gave an exaggerated sigh. "What I mean is, where'd they come from?"

Pogo opened his baggie and ate a Vanilla Bloom as an avalanche of crumbs rolled down his t-shirt.

Jack took a step back so the crumbs wouldn't land on his tennis shoes. "I made them. With Theo Porter."

"Why?" Pogo asked, wiping his mouth with the back of his hand.

"Because it's my new hobby. Theo helped me get started."

Pogo leaned in and whispered, "Isn't baking for girls?"

Carlos smacked his arm. "What century are you living in, Pogodinski?"

"Girls can hunt, and guys can bake," Jack replied.

"Just kidding, dude. Sorry." Pogo shoved a Cocoroon in his mouth and gagged a little.

"You don't like it?" Jack said, startled.

"Coconut is gross. No offense."

Carlos pointed to his cookies. "Then I'll trade you these frilly white things—"

"They're called Vanilla Blooms," Jack interjected.

"Right. I'll trade you my Vanilla Blooms for your—"

"Cocoroons," Jack supplied.

"How about it, then?" Carlos said to Pogo.

"Deal," Pogo answered, and there was a shuffling of cookies.

Carlos sniffed one of the Cocoroons. "Are they poisonous?"

"If they were poisonous, I'd be dead by now," Pogo said.

"Good point." Carlos took a bite, and his brown eyes widened. "Not bad."

Jack took that as a compliment and was ready to thank Carlos, but he was knocked to the side by someone walking past them. He turned to see who it was.

Benny grunted. "You again."

"*You* again," Jack replied, but he was instantly distracted by the *thing* in Benny's hand. "What is *that*?"

Marvelous Jackson

"That's *sick*!" Pogo said.

Benny glowed. "It's a lower jawbone."

"Benny, have you gone and murdered someone with your hockey stick?" Carlos asked.

Benny waved his hand in front of Carlos as if to say *buzz off*.

"Is that thing real?" Jack said.

"I wish. It's just a plastic model." The silver wire in Benny's mouth flickered.

"Since when are you into teeth?" Carlos asked.

"Since Wilson knocked out my incisor in this very hallway," Benny retorted.

Jack cringed.

"By the way, I changed my science experiment to a project on molars, which is *way* more interesting than ocean creatures, if you ask me," Benny said.

"I *didn't* ask—" Pogo started to say, but Jack nudged him so he'd shut up.

No fights, no arguments. Not with me anywhere in the vicinity, he thought.

Benny gestured at the cookies that Carlos and Pogo were holding. "I hope you brush your teeth after eating all that sugar. It's not good for your enamel." He turned and left.

"What was *that* all about?" Pogo murmured.

"Girls can hunt, guys can bake, and apparently, Benny is capable of surprising us all." Jack was certain that he and Benny would never like each other, but he smiled as he said the words.

Seventeen
Lunkers

As Jack let himself inside the cottage, his phone lit up with Rusty's number. Why was Rusty calling him? The first thing that flew into Jack's mind was *What if something's wrong with Norm?*

He couldn't bear it if his dad had gotten sick, injured, or worse. Sure, he and Norm hadn't exactly been *close* as of late, but the thought of being a complete orphan made him want to throw up.

He answered the call as fast as he could.

"Jackal! What's up?" Rusty yelled in his ear.

"Nothing. Are you guys OK?"

"Everything's dandy. I'm calling because your old man wants to know if you're free."

"Free for what?"

"You mentioned something about doing nuggie intel, and he's very interested."

Jack laughed. "Yeah, I'm free for nuggie intel, but can Norm pull himself away from Dutch's for an hour or two?"

"He's leaving me and Dusty in charge, which he's never done before," Rusty replied, and Jack heard a note of pride in his voice. "He'll pick you up in a little while. Ope, I gotta run, Jackal. The Vogel brothers just came in for today's special."

"Three heaping platters of Braunschweiger and potato hash coming right up!" Dusty shouted in the background. "I hope Bobb, Nedd, and Lloyd are hungry!"

Rusty clicked off, and Jack searched the cottage for his baseball hat. It almost didn't fit over his overgrown hair, but he smooshed it down until it stayed in place.

Norm is leaving Dutch's!

Nothing like that had happened in four hundred and eighty-something days.

Or was it four hundred and *ninety*-something days?

Jack wondered if the running tally in his head needed a new battery.

Or maybe it's just time to let go of it.

He realized how tired he was from all that counting.

...

Jack watched an episode of *MMKBC* while he waited for Norm to pick him up. He'd set a big goal of catching up on all the seasons he'd missed.

Marvelous Jackson

He hummed along to the show's theme song, which featured trilling flutes, brassy trumpets, and a catchy drumbeat. Just hearing the music made his stomach flutter.

One episode became two, and two became three, and Jack began to wonder if Norm hadn't been able to tear himself away from Dutch's after all. He realized how much he'd been looking forward to spending time with him, even if it was just for a nuggie reconnaissance mission.

You coming to get me? he texted Norm.

No reply.

He frowned and turned his attention back to *MMKBC*.

One of the contestants was frosting a dozen peanut butter cupcakes with silky chocolate ganache. Her name was Ellie, and Jack wondered how her cupcakes would hold up during her critique. They looked pretty, but Shane O'Shaughnessy had banned eggs for the challenge, so Ellie had used ripe bananas as a replacement.

"I think the bananas will have a nice binding effect in my batter," she told the camera. "Just like eggs."

"A nice binding effect," Jack repeated. He loved it when contestants said things like that.

Norm's horn blasted from the driveway.

He's here!

Jack jumped up, switched off the television, and jogged outside.

"Hi," Norm said as Jack climbed inside the pickup truck.

"Hi."

Norm pointed at Jack's baseball hat. "How on earth did you manage to get that thing on over your hair?"

"It wasn't easy, but it was necessary. Top secret mission and all." Jack grinned.

Norm grinned back. "Tell me about this nuggie intel you've got up your sleeve."

"Which restaurant is Dutch's biggest competition for the nuggie contest?" Jack asked.

Norm didn't hesitate. "Lunkers Table and Tap, for sure."

"Lunkers it is. Let's go."

When they arrived at Lunkers, Jack told Norm to park in the spot that was farthest away from the door.

"Why does it matter?" Norm said.

"Because we can't risk you being seen. Not only are you the getaway driver, but you're the owner of Lunkers's rival restaurant."

Norm tilted his head. "You can't be serious."

"Of course I'm serious! Now stay here. Keep out of sight. I'll be back soon."

Jack got out of the truck, pulled the bill of his baseball hat down as low as it would go, and went inside.

"Hiya, hon," said the Lunkers hostess. She wore a nametag that said *Lorraine*.

Marvelous Jackson

"Hello. I'd like to order takeout for supper."

Lorraine handed Jack an oversized menu with thick, laminated pages. "Hope you can read this with your cap covering your eyes."

"I'll be fine." Jack moved off to the side so he could take his time scanning the entrees. There was no mention of nuggies, but that didn't surprise him. *Because who's stupid enough to serve their nuggies to the public and thus give away all their secrets this close to the competition?*

Jack *did* see that chicken tenders, chicken fingers, and chicken drummies were listed on the menu. *Perfect.* He went back to the hostess stand and told Lorraine he was ready to order.

She took out a pen and pad of paper from her apron pocket. "What name should I place the order under, hon?"

"Um . . ." For a split second, Jack's mind went blank. "Sally."

"Well, you don't look like a Sally now, do ya?"

"She's my . . . aunt."

"All righty, Sally's nephew, what'll you have?"

Jack ordered the chicken tenders, chicken fingers, and chicken drummies.

"You sure do like chicken!" Lorraine exclaimed.

"I guess you could say that," Jack mumbled. He added a side salad and a basket of tater tots to shake things up, and then he took a deep breath for courage. "Lorraine, can I please ask you a few questions about your menu items?"

"Fire away."

"Aunt Sally wants to know what kind of oil you fry your chicken in. She's got . . . food allergies. You know, digestive problems."

Lorraine nodded. "We fry everything in sunflower oil."

"What's in your breading?"

"Flour, garlic powder, and ground mustard."

"How about your marinade?"

"Well, aren't you Mister Million Questions!" Lorraine chuckled and leaned toward Jack. "Between you and me, I think Lunkers is real lazy when it comes to marinade, but no one around here cares what I think. I'm just the hostess."

Jack smiled sweetly. "*I* care what you think."

"Thanks, hon. We just throw together soy sauce and lemon juice. That's it."

"It sounds like Aunt Sally will be OK, then."

"What a relief. You wanna pay now or when your food's ready?" Lorraine asked.

"Now is fine."

Lorraine rang up the order, but it occurred to Jack that he didn't have one cent on him. He patted his pockets sheepishly. "I have to run out to the car to grab money from . . . Aunt Sally. I'll be right back."

Marvelous Jackson

At the truck, he tapped on Norm's window.

Norm rolled it down. "Done already? Where's the food?"

"I need money."

Norm dug in his back pocket for his wallet and handed Jack a credit card, but Jack shook his head. "We can't use that. Your name is printed right on it. We need cash."

"Right." Norm gave Jack some bills, and Jack went back inside.

Lorraine counted out his change. "You go to school nearby, hon? Evergreen? Boulder Bay?"

"No . . . I'm visiting Aunt Sally from Madison," Jack replied. He hoped his cheeks weren't pink from all the lies rolling off his tongue.

"That explains why I've never seen you here before."

"Exactly," Jack murmured. *Hardly!* he thought. *The son of the owner of Dutch's would never be caught dead eating at Lunkers Table and Tap!*

Jack stood off to the side to wait for his food, which Lorraine said would take a few minutes. The restaurant door opened, and a man walked in.

Jack would recognize that nose anywhere.

Principal Engel!

If Principal Engel noticed him, Jack was toast. He would give away Jack's identity, and Jack would look like a complete idiot in front of Lorraine. Even worse, his failed nuggie mission would cast a big, dark shadow over Dutch's—and his dad.

Jack leaned over to tie his left shoe, even though it didn't need tying.

Then he tied his right shoe, because Principal Engel and Lorraine were now chatting leisurely about the weather, the approaching holiday season, and the nuggie competition.

At the mention of "nuggie competition," Jack's ears perked up.

He went back to his left shoe and tied the laces *again*. He would stay in this position as long as he needed to, even though blood was beginning to pool in his head.

"Is Lunkers ready to compete?" Principal Engel asked Lorraine.

"I think so, but between you and me, I wish we had a better marinade," she said.

"Who's your biggest rival?"

"Dutch's. But from what I hear, those guys don't use ground mustard in their batter, which I think is a mortal sin."

Upside down, Jack scoffed.

After what felt like hours, Lorraine finally spirited Principal Engel away to a table, and Jack unfolded his body. He was sure that his face was as red as an undercooked steak.

Lorraine returned to the hostess stand with two plastic bags. "Here's your supper. Hot and fresh for ya, hon."

Marvelous Jackson

Jack thanked her and took the bags. Steam snuck out of the containers and tickled his hands.

"Stop by next time you're up from Madison!" Lorraine called out.

"I sure will," Jack said. *Not a chance*, he thought.

He went outside, climbed in the truck, and set the bags between him and Norm. "Our nuggie mission is complete," he announced.

Norm cheered.

Eighteen
Flavor Profile

"How was it?" Norm bounced in his seat like a little kid. "Did you get any good intel?"

"I got a *lot* of good intel," Jack replied. "Among other things, I learned that Lunkers uses ground mustard in their batter, and that their marinade is underwhelming—just soy sauce and lemon juice, if you can believe that."

Norm stared at him. "How'd you find all that out?"

Jack grinned. "Just one of my talents, I guess."

Norm went to open one of the carryout bags, but Jack told him that they needed to leave.

"Leave? Why?"

"Even though it's dark out, we can't risk being seen or getting caught." Jack thought of Principal Engel eating inside the restaurant. "Let's go to Thimbleberry Park. It's close enough, and while you drive, I'll tell you everything the hostess leaked to me."

Jack talked the whole way there, and Norm listened to every word.

After pulling into Thimbleberry Park's empty lot, Norm turned off the truck, flicked on the interior lights, and slid everything out of the bags.

"I know that chicken tenders, fingers, and drummies aren't the same thing as chicken nuggies, but it was the best I could do," Jack said. "At the very least, we can get a better sense of Lunkers's flavor profile."

"Did you just say *flavor profile*?"

Jack shrugged. "I learned it from watching *MMKBC*."

"What in the world is *MMKBC*?"

"*The Marvelous Midwest Kids Baking Championship*."

"You're really stuck on this baking thing, huh?"

Jack nodded.

"But you'd be so good—"

"I *know* I'd be so good at cooking. But baking and cooking aren't all that different, really, and you've already taught me a lot about being in the kitchen and using good ingredients. I just prefer making sweet things."

"Fair enough." Norm stroked the bristly hairs on his jaw. "I mean, it'd be a thrill for me to watch you roast a turkey or assemble a killer Reuben, but I know your mom would be happy that you're doing something she enjoyed so much."

Jack loved hearing Norm say the words, because he'd been thinking the same thing.

"Remember the time she made chocolate chip cookies and went to her shift at the library without realizing she'd sat in dough?" Norm chuckled. "Jean Ann noticed the splotch on the back of her white jeans, and they couldn't stop laughing. A patron complained because they were making so much noise."

Jack would never get sick of reminiscing about his mom. He laughed along with Norm, until his stomach gave a noisy growl.

"Guess we should eat now—" The words were barely out of Norm's mouth before Jack tore into the carryout containers.

They passed the chicken back and forth, munching, swallowing, and wiping the grease from their fingers with flimsy paper napkins.

"The texture of this drummy isn't crunchy enough," Jack said, a few minutes later. "It's too oily."

Norm nodded. "Not to mention the ground mustard is totally overrated."

Jack examined the drummy up close and wished he had a magnifying glass like Vicky Willow. "There's not enough black pepper. You need to have some visible specks in your batter, because it makes the finished product look more interesting."

"At least the drummy is moist, because nobody likes dry chicken," Norm said.

Marvelous Jackson

Jack speared a plastic forkful of salad and made a face as he chewed. "Lunkers would get in big trouble for their wilted iceberg lettuce, soggy croutons, and bland dressing. *You've been burned. Put away your rolling pin because you're going home.*"

Norm chuckled. "What does *that* mean?"

"It's what Shane O'Shaughnessy says at the end of *MMKBC*, when he's booting off the contestant who's just lost the challenge."

Norm chuckled again.

"Hey, do you want to do nuggie intel again sometime?" Jack asked. He couldn't believe how much fun he was having.

"Honestly, I'm not sure we need to, buddy," Norm answered. "I was thinking Lunkers would be our biggest adversary. I don't mean to sound heartless, but I'm not sure their chicken is anything special after all."

"Right," Jack replied, trying not to sound disappointed. He would've leapt at the chance to run another sneaky errand with Norm. If that's what it took to reconnect with his dad, he'd do it in a heartbeat.

"We *do* need to punch up our own nuggie recipe, though," Norm went on. "I feel like we're still missing an ingredient or two."

"I can help with that. Do you think—"

Norm's phone rang. "Sorry, I gotta get this. It's Dusty. Maybe something's come up at Dutch's."

There's always something coming up at Dutch's, Jack thought.

Norm listened to Dusty for a minute or two before he started hollering, "You're telling me there wasn't *one slice* of bacon in that huge shipment we got earlier? Yes, yes, like you said, I'm sure you and Rusty have things *totally under control*, but I'll be there right away."

Jack could imagine Dusty protesting on the other line.

"I said, *I'll be there right away*." With a huff, Norm turned on the truck.

Jack's sigh was inaudible under the rumble of the engine. When the nuggie competition was over, would Norm ever pay attention to him again? Jack wasn't sure how they would bridge the distance that stretched between them if Norm was always so focused on Dutch's.

Norm pulled out of the parking lot, and just like that, their outing came to an end.

Nineteen
Illinois, Indiana, Iowa, Kansas, Michigan, Minnesota, Missouri, Nebraska, North Dakota, Ohio, South Dakota, Wisconsin

As soon as Jack returned to the cottage, he flopped onto the couch. His night with Norm had been cut short, but at least he could pick up his *MMKBC* episode where he'd left off.

The judges began their critiques of Ellie's cupcakes.

"Your idea of substituting mashed bananas for eggs was brilliant," Archie Gomez told her.

"They certainly created a lovely binding effect," Vicky Willow added.

Ellie is amazing, Jack thought. It wasn't just her mashed bananas that were impressive. She brought so many skills and talents to the competition, he couldn't help but tick through them all.

First off, Ellie had good time management. When Shane O'Shaughnessy blew his golden whistle to start a challenge, she closed her eyes and made a point of planning out how she would use every minute allotted to her.

She measured her ingredients with precision. Case in point: Jack had never seen her add too much sugar or not enough salt.

She followed the rules. If Shane O'Shaughnessy told the contestants to bake an Italian orange sponge cake, that's exactly what she did.

She came up with flavor profiles no one else thought of—like putting dried cranberries, fresh pear slices, and black pepper in her scone mix. She'd raised some eyebrows with that combination, but it had worked.

She stayed calm, even as the kitchen heated up and the challenges became stressful. *Which means you never see her throwing flaming-hot cookie sheets across the room when she burns something*, Jack thought.

Finally, Ellie was just plain *nice*. When Vicky Willow and Archie Gomez judged her, she listened quietly and never got defensive or angry. She always congratulated the winner and hugged the loser.

In Jack's opinion, Ellie was flawless. He wasn't aiming for perfection himself, but he knew he could learn a lot by watching her and trying out her strategies.

Marvelous Jackson

MMKBC cut to a commercial break, and Shane O'Shaughnessy's face filled the television screen. "Are you an aspiring baker?" he asked.

"Yep," Jack replied.

"Are you ten to thirteen years old?"

"Yep."

"Are you from Illinois, Indiana, Iowa, Kansas, Michigan, Minnesota, Missouri, Nebraska, North Dakota, Ohio, South Dakota, or Wisconsin?" Shane O'Shaughnessy listed off the states so effortlessly, it sounded like they were one entity: *Illinoisindianaiowakansasmichiganminnesota missourinebraskanorthdakotaohiosouthdakotawisconsin.*

"Yep."

"Do you do well under pressure?"

"I'm working on it."

"Are you interested in auditioning to become a contestant for the next season of *The Marvelous Midwest Kids Baking Championship*?"

Jack had been so enamored of *MMKBC*'s past seasons, it hadn't occurred to him that there would be *future* seasons as well.

"Well?" Shane O'Shaughnessy demanded. He seemed to be talking directly to Jack. "Are you interested?"

Jack had never thought about it before, but the answer was obvious.

"Yes."

He launched himself off the couch and, in a frenzy, pushed the hair out of his eyes.

He couldn't deny it. He wanted to audition to be a contestant on the next season of *MMKBC*!

Shane O'Shaughnessy went on. "Apply online, and maybe you'll be chosen to come to the Windy City to audition in person. Tell us about your baking successes! Tell us about your baking catastrophes! We can't wait to hear from you! Don't delay! Apply now!"

Jack wondered if Shane O'Shaughnessy only spoke in sentences that ended in exclamation points.

MMKBC's website flashed across the screen before Shane O'Shaughnessy's gleaming white teeth disappeared and a commercial for dog food began.

Chicago!

Don't delay!

Apply now!

Feverishly, Jack unzipped his backpack and yanked out his laptop.

Twenty
Only Chance

Jack skimmed the instructions that were listed on *MMKBC*'s website.

"No way," he moaned. "The application is due by midnight *tonight*."

It was already eight o'clock.

Part of him was thrilled that the deadline hadn't already passed, but the other part was freaked out that midnight was just four hours away.

If Jack had started watching *MMKBC* sooner—like *way* before Theo had invited him over to his cottage—he would've seen the commercial earlier, which would've given him weeks or even months to get his application together. He ran his hands through his hair, making it stick straight up. There was no way he could apply in such a short amount of time.

I'm not an experienced baker anyway, he thought, trying to make himself feel better. *The show would never want someone like me.*

He shut his laptop with a hopeless click just as his phone buzzed.

Clare: Hi, what's up?

Jack: Not much, you?

Clare: Nothing

Jack: Actually, I lied, there IS something up

Jack told Clare about the *MMKBC* commercial he'd just seen and how it was messing with his head.

Clare: Well, why don't you apply?

Jack: I can't put an application together by midnight! Plus, I'm a new baker, I'm still figuring out how to do it without my mom . . .

Marvelous Jackson

His phone rang.

"What do you mean you can't put an application together by midnight?" Clare yelled in his ear. "You *have* to. I love that show!"

Jack couldn't believe she was actually calling him. "I love it, too," he managed to say. "But even if I *did* figure out a way to apply by midnight, *MMKBC* would never pick me to audition."

"Why would you say that?"

"Because there's so much about baking that I don't know. I'm still a beginner."

"If you don't apply, I'll go online myself and pretend to be you. I'll submit an application in your name," Clare said.

He laughed. "Yeah, right."

"Come on." She sounded serious. "You owe it to yourself. You're thirteen, right? That's the oldest a contestant can be. It's your only chance."

"I guess." Jack chewed his lip.

"Just give it a try," she said, as if she'd made the decision for him. "You've got nothing to lose."

Jack relented. "Fine. I'll take a look at the application."

"I'm hanging up now so you can get started. There's not one minute to spare."

"OK—" Jack said, but she was already gone.

...

Back on his laptop, Jack clicked the *APPLY FOR THE NEXT SEASON OF THE MARVELOUS MIDWEST KIDS BAKING CHAMPIONSHIP* button, which took him to a page of questions.

He filled in the blanks with his name, age, birthday, grade, school, and hometown. He had to explain how long he'd been baking, and what his favorite recipe was.

When he reached the bottom of the screen, he smiled smugly. It was only nine o'clock. The application hadn't even taken him an hour! He clicked *SUBMIT*.

Except—there was more.

A whole new screen popped up. *APPLICATION: PART TWO.*

Jack wondered how many parts there were.

He read the instructions and groaned. "A video? I have to submit a video of myself talking?"

Unlike everyone else at Evergreen, who didn't mind posting videos of themselves online, Jack was *not* eager to gush about himself in front of a camera. He couldn't remember the last time he'd showered. And all his hoodies were dirty.

But he knew he was just making excuses.

He ransacked his closet for any article of clothing that was remotely clean. Attached to a crooked wire hanger was a button-down shirt he hadn't worn since his mom's funeral. He put it on and frowned. The sleeves were three inches too short, and the hemline hovered above his belly

Marvelous Jackson

button, but he had no other options. He'd have to make sure that his head was the only thing visible on-screen.

He scrubbed his face and used a squirt of hair gel so his eyes wouldn't be hidden behind his scraggly mane.

When there was nothing else he could do about his appearance, he sat at the kitchen table with his laptop in front of him.

He reviewed the website's instructions one more time. He had to talk about what he was like as a person, how baking had impacted his life, and why he wanted to be on *MMKBC*.

Speak naturally! the website said, using as many exclamation points as Shane O'Shaughnessy himself. *We want to get a sense of your vibe! Be you!*

Jack switched on the camera and briefly admired his hair.

"You clean up good. Now, don't make yourself sound like a jerk."

He began to record.

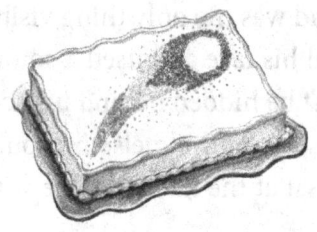

Twenty-One
A Big Hello to Shane, Vicky, and Archie

Jack's mouth grew dry from talking so much, but he didn't stop.

Finally, he reached the end of his rambling. "In summary, I hope you'll invite me to Chicago to audition. I'm thirteen years old, so this is my only chance to try out. Thank you for your time, and please give a big hello to Shane, Vicky, and Archie for me."

Jack stopped the video and scowled.

"Did I really just say '*Give a big hello to Shane, Vicky, and Archie for me*'?"

He made a puking noise and considered deleting everything he'd just recorded, but he couldn't afford to do it all over again. It was now ten o'clock, and Norm could walk in the door at any minute. Jack didn't want to tell him about his *MMKBC* application. If he wasn't chosen, Norm would be none the wiser; but if he was, what a great surprise it would be.

Jack clicked *SUBMIT*.

Except—there was more.

A whole new screen popped up. *APPLICATION: PART THREE.*

"Part *three*? Are you kidding me?"

He wanted to cry.

"I need to bake, frost, and decorate an entire cake?"

It should be an imaginative cake that represents who you are as a person, the website explained.

Show off your creativity! Prove that you've got what it takes to be on our show! Snap and download some photographs of your cake and describe what you like most about it. How is it special? How is it original?

Jack had never baked a cake by himself, so he'd have to figure it out—and fast. He'd come too far to give up now.

He still had his cookbooks from the library, so he flipped through them until he found a recipe for a simple sheet cake. It didn't look fancy, but he could pour all his energy into decorating it. Thanks to the Porters, he was well stocked with sprinkles. He hoped they would set his cake apart from everybody else's.

Jack pulled flour, sugar, and oil from the pantry as he channeled his very best Shane O'Shaughnessy. "Your time starts right now!" he bellowed at the top of his lungs.

...

Jack stirred a bowl of white icing and licked some of it off the spoon. Not bad for his first try.

He began to frost the cake—which he prayed was cool enough—in rapid, careful strokes. To his relief, the icing didn't melt or clump. There was no room for mistakes, because it was now eleven fifteen. His application was due in forty-five minutes.

Jack picked through the jars of **Golden Chips, Razzle Dazzles, and Baby Beach Balls and sorted** all the red, white, and blue sprinkles into three separate piles. It was a fussy, painstaking task, and he hoped it would be worth it in the end.

He steadied his wrist and began to scatter red sprinkles in the bottom left corner of the cake. The red sprinkles transitioned into white, and the white sprinkles transitioned into blue.

By the time he got to the upper right corner, Jack had created a red, white, and blue meteor streaking across an alabaster sky. It was his own interpretation of the American flag. He decided to call it Presidential Pride.

He photographed the cake and uploaded the pictures to his laptop.

By now, it was eleven thirty, and there were *still* more questions to answer.

His fingers flew across the keyboard.

Marvelous Jackson

Keep going. Faster, faster. You don't have much—
Outside, a car door slammed.
Oh, no.
Norm was home!
Jack wiped a bead of sweat off his nose.

Fleetingly, he considered stowing the cake in his bedroom, but there was no way he could hide the fact that he'd been baking. After all, the sink was piled high with dirty pans, the floor was covered in runaway sprinkles, and the cottage smelled just like a sugar factory.

He left the cake right where it was on the table.

Norm walked in, his shoulders drooping with exhaustion. "Hi, buddy. Why aren't you in bed?" He sniffed, and his face brightened. "Hey, have you been baking?"

"Yep." It was eleven forty-five. Jack couldn't afford to get into a conversation right now. He slid his laptop under his arm and started backing out of the kitchen.

"Why on earth are you wearing a button-down shirt? That thing doesn't fit you anymore."

"You're absolutely right," Jack replied. He had to get out of there to finish his application! Precious time was ticking away.

Norm noticed the cake on the table. "Hey, is this what you made?"

From the doorway, Jack nodded. Two more inches, and he'd be out of the kitchen.

Norm smacked his lips. "Would you mind if I tried a little? I'm still stuffed from all that chicken we ate from Lunkers, but I'd sure love a midnight snack."

"Go ahead," Jack said, trying to sound chill. "I need to go to bed."

"Aren't you going to clean up this mess first?"

"First thing in the morning, I promise. I'm just really tired."

"I hear ya. I'm beat, too. First thing tomorrow, then. Sleep tight." Norm yawned and cut into the Presidential Pride.

Jack dashed into his bedroom and leaped onto his bed. His body buzzed with fatigue and adrenaline as he finished typing every single thing he needed to say.

Right at 11:59, he clicked what he prayed was the final *SUBMIT* button.

He couldn't breathe. What if he'd missed a part of the application? What if there was *another* unexpected task he needed to complete? He'd be out of luck, because it was too late to do anything else.

His hands were slimy. He wiped them on his jeans and waited to see if the last four hours had been for nothing.

A message popped up on the screen, and Jack gasped.

> *Thank you for your interest in auditioning for the next season of* THE MARVELOUS MIDWEST KIDS BAKING CHAMPIONSHIP! *We've received*

all the parts of your application, and we'll let you know very soon if you've been chosen to audition in Chicago. Good luck and keep baking.

He tipped over in a relieved, sweaty heap on his mattress.

I did it!

Twenty-Two
That Boy with the Cake

The following morning, Jack's phone buzzed with a text. He peeled his eyelids open and saw that it was from Clare. Despite his tiredness, he grinned.

Clare
Did you submit your application?

Jack
Yes, at the very last minute, and I mean literally

Clare
Was it hard?

Jack sent Clare photos of his Presidential Pride.

Marvelous Jackson

Jack

YES, you could say it was hard! I had to bake a cake as part of it!

Clare

But it turned out so pretty. When do you hear back from the show?

Jack

The website said VERY SOON, whatever that means

Clare

Jack padded into the kitchen to take care of the mess he'd made the night before—but everything had already been washed, dried, and swept. He gaped at the spotless floors and shiny countertops.

Norm must've cleaned up for him.

But he was so tired from work, Jack thought.

Norm had devoured half of the Presidential Pride and left a note next to it:

> *I thought you might like feedback on your cake. It's a little salty, but not too much. The middle is fluffy,*

but the edges are crunchy. (Not sure why?) Great job decorating. Sorry I ate so much. It was really good. I cleaned up the kitchen to show my thanks.

Norm's critique sounded like it belonged on an episode of *MMKBC*. Jack grinned. Even if he didn't get an audition for the show, he had earned his dad's support.

On his phone, he searched the internet for "*Overcooked edges of cake*" and found that he'd probably used too much grease in his pan.

"Cool," he murmured.

He was still learning. It wouldn't happen again.

...

After school, Jack parked his bike in the woods and went inside the library. He dropped his cookbooks in the return bin and handed a container of Presidential Pride to Miss Jean Ann, who was perched behind the circulation desk.

She removed the lid and sniffed. "What's this?"

"It's a cake. I made it."

"Your mom would've loved the red, white, and blue."

"That's what I was going for," Jack said. "I found the recipe in one of the cookbooks I checked out, but I came up with the decorations all on my own. I think the cake's a little salty, and the edges are too crunchy, but I hope you like it anyway."

"Of course I'll like it," Miss Jean Ann retorted as she admired the Presidential Pride.

An older lady poked her head out of the librarians' office. "May I borrow you for a moment, Miss Jean Ann? I need assistance with a box of periodicals." She was small and bony, and her hair floated above her head like a puff of steel wool.

Was Jack imagining it, or did she narrow her eyes at him?

"That's Miss Holzhacker," Miss Jean Ann whispered to Jack. "**She's our new library volunteer. She's a retired schoolteacher who likes to stay busy.** *Very* **busy.**"

"I can help with the box of periodicals if you want me to," Jack offered.

"I think we're good for now, but thanks for volunteering," Miss Jean Ann said as she disappeared into the office.

In the stacks, Jack grabbed a cookbook from the shelf and sat in his now-familiar spot on the carpet. He wondered if he would make a flattened-out patch there, too. He flipped to the dessert chapter and began reading.

Lemon bars. Pecan sticky buns. Cookie cups.

He wanted to make them all.

Next, he searched the cookbook for anything involving chicken. Norm was still hoping to punch up his nuggies a little bit, and Jack wanted to help. He found a recipe called *FRIED FINGERS YOU WON'T FORGET*, and his eyes widened as he reviewed the list of ingredients.

Dill pickle juice in the marinade?
Confectioners' sugar in the batter?

He didn't know ingredients like that could be used in a chicken recipe! He couldn't wait to tell Norm. When he finished up at the library, he would bike directly to Dutch's, where he could eat supper and share what he'd learned.

The ceiling lights of the library flicked on and off a couple hours later, and Jack couldn't believe how fast the evening had passed.

"Ten minutes until closing," Miss Holzhacker announced over the loudspeaker. "I repeat, ten minutes until closing."

Jack reshelved the cookbooks he'd been reading. As he walked toward the lobby, a voice floated through the air. "That boy with the cake, who stopped by the circulation desk earlier . . ."

He froze.

The voice belonged to Miss Holzhacker.

"He reminds me of someone. He reminds me of . . . trouble."

Jack opened his mouth in protest. *Is she talking about me? She doesn't even know me!*

Miss Jean Ann shushed her. "His name is Jackson, and he's a lovely young man, Miss Holzhacker."

Marvelous Jackson

She really IS talking about me, Jack thought. The muscles across his back tensed.

"But he reminds me of someone," Miss Holzhacker insisted once again.

Who do I remind her of? Jack shouted in his head. *I've never met this lady before tonight!*

"Jackson is trying to find his way after going through a very difficult time," Miss Jean Ann said in a firm voice he'd never heard before.

The contrast between Miss Jean Ann's compassion and Miss Holzhacker's contempt caught Jack off guard, and he was blinded by tears, hot and thick as soup. He stumbled into the men's restroom, which was just off the lobby. He locked himself in a stall and tried to muffle the sound of his crying.

He thought about how kind Miss Jean Ann was, and how *unkind* Miss Holzhacker was, for no apparent reason at all. He'd never done anything to bother her.

But as his sniffles subsided and his head cleared, Jack couldn't deny that he had said mean things to other people, too.

Like when he'd teased Benny for having a head the size and shape of a watermelon.

And when he'd told his whole gym class that Rebecca Danner's lip gloss looked as sticky as fly paper.

And—worst of all—when he'd made fun of Lola and Theo for having two moms.

Never again will I be a jerk like that, he vowed.

The patter of footsteps made its way toward the men's bathroom. "Library's closing," Miss Holzhacker called out. Jack took a seat on the toilet and lifted both his feet off the ground. He needed to conceal himself. He wasn't ready to face her.

The restroom door flew open.

"Library's closing!"

Jack couldn't believe how *extreme* she was. He scrunched up his face.

After a beat of silence, Miss Holzhacker's shoes squeaked as she turned to leave. The door started to shut behind her, but at the same moment, Jack's phone buzzed with a text. He switched it to silent mode as fast as he could, but not before Miss Holzhacker poked her head back in the restroom. "Is someone in here?" she hissed.

Leave me alone! he thought.

To Jack's horror, she began checking the stalls, one by one.

Now he'd have to pretend that he was actually *using* the toilet, which would be outrageously embarrassing. But just as Miss Holzhacker approached the stall Jack was in, someone called out from the hallway, requesting help with an overdue book.

"I can certainly renew your book," Miss Holzhacker replied to the patron. "But perhaps you shouldn't have allowed it to become overdue in the first place." The

Marvelous Jackson

men's bathroom door clumped shut, and the unbearable squealing of her shoes receded.

Jack blew his nose and thought about how nice it would be to sleep over at the library again. He could stay right where he was until Miss Holzhacker and Miss Jean Ann locked up for the night, and then he could sneak out and relax on the whistle chairs under the card catalog.

It would make me so happy, he thought. *And no one would ever know I was here.*

After all, his bedroom door was closed, and his bike was safe in the woods.

I wouldn't make a mess or get into anything.

Jack pictured his mom's face on the plaque in the lobby, just steps from where he was hiding. She had smiled down at him the first time he'd trespassed at the library, when it was a complete accident, but this time would be different. He knew she wouldn't be pleased with his decision.

Jack checked his phone and saw that it was Norm who'd texted a few minutes before and almost gotten him busted.

I'm thinking about that dandy of a cake you made, Norm had written. *I don't say it enough (or ever?), but I'm real proud of you, buddy.*

Jack went limp.

What am I doing? he wondered.

He knew that sleeping at the library wasn't a good idea at all.

He'd been on a roll with his good behavior, and he didn't want to jeopardize it. If he got caught, Norm would never trust him again.

I have to get out of here before it's too late!

He unlocked the stall door and tiptoed out of the men's room.

Miss Holzhacker and Miss Jean Ann were somewhere in the library, turning off lights. They hadn't locked the front door yet, so Jack made a run for it. With shaky limbs, he darted into the night.

He snuck around the side of the library to fetch his bike. He'd barely entered the dark, silent woods when Miss Jean Ann and Miss Holzhacker walked out the employee door. He crouched down as they got in their cars and drove away.

That was close, he thought.

He was getting ready to stand up when a *different* car pulled into the lot.

Headlights swooped over Jack as he dropped to the ground and pressed himself into the dirt. His mind raced. Who would be arriving at the library so late? Did someone know he was there? Could he get in trouble just for *considering* making a bad choice?

He listened to the slamming of doors and the hum of voices. He heard the clinking of keys and the thud of the employee entrance. The lights flicked back on inside the library and sent a warm yellow glow across the parking lot. He was just deep enough in the woods that the light didn't quite reach him.

Jack sat up and pulled a twig from his hair. His jeans and hoodie were damp and smelled like mold. He peered through the trees at a white van with the words *ENERGETIC EARL'S EXCELLENT JANITORIAL SERVICE* on the side.

"Holy cow," he whispered.

If he had stayed at the library, he would've gotten caught by janitors.

As quietly as possible, Jack put on his helmet and wheeled his bike through the woods, hoping Earl and his crew wouldn't hear the snapping of sticks and branches that accompanied him.

When he finally got to the road, he leaped onto his bike and started to pedal, faster than he'd ever pedaled before. Quickly, soundlessly, he rode toward Dutch's, his dad, and a nuggie recipe he was **one hundred percent** confident he could improve.

Twenty-Three
What's in this Chicken?

"Yo, Jackal!" Rusty said when Jack walked into Dutch's. "Looks like you've been spending some quality time in nature. You all right?"

Jack extracted a small leaf from the crown of his head. "Yep."

"What are you doing here so late, Jacky?" Dusty was wearing one of his plaid lumberjack shirts, and he had a pencil tucked behind his ear.

"I wanted to get something to eat for supper, if you guys still have stuff out." Jack sat down on a stool. "Also, I've got some new ideas to share about our nuggie recipe."

"We've always got stuff out, and we love new ideas." With a metal spatula, Rusty pointed to the burgers he was flipping on the grill. "Want one?"

Marvelous Jackson

Jack nodded. "With American cheese."

"Please?" Rusty said.

"Please," Jack replied. "And thank you."

"That's better."

A few minutes later, Rusty set a burger in front of him, along with a mound of salty fries.

Norm walked in from the dining room and grinned when he saw Jack. "At Dutch's again, buddy? Seems like you just can't stay away."

Jack held up his hands. "I'm here by choice, not to be babysat. There's a big difference."

"Fair enough. You got my text?"

Jack nodded. "It was nice. Thanks." *Even if it almost got me in trouble with the meanest lady I've ever met.*

Norm wiped Jack's cheek with his thumb. "Why is there dried mud on your face?"

"No idea," Jack lied, picturing the rotten undergrowth of the woods next to the library. "Hey, I've been doing some nuggie research."

Norm looked at him expectantly. "Really?"

"Have you ever considered using pickle juice in your marinade?" Jack shoved a fry in his mouth.

"Pickle juice?" Norm, Dusty, and Rusty said at the same time.

"What about confectioners' sugar in your batter? Have you ever thought about that?"

"You can't be serious, Jacky." Dusty pulled a pad of

paper from his apron and wrote furiously with the pencil that had been lodged behind his ear.

"I'm totally serious," Jack said. "I found a recipe in a cookbook, and I thought pickle juice and confectioners' sugar sounded cool. The author went on and on about how much flavor they add. He said that everybody who eats it will demand to know, *What's in this chicken?*"

"Who wrote the cookbook?" Norm asked. "Please tell me it's not a chef from around here. I can't incorporate any ideas that somebody else might use."

Jack had read all about the author on the back flap of the cookbook. "He's a chef named Kelly Clinton, and he's from Connecticut, so I doubt he'll be entering a nuggie competition in northern Wisconsin."

Norm, Rusty, and Dusty exhaled.

"You're *intense*, Jacky." Dusty tucked the pencil behind his ear again. "And I approve."

Rusty gave a loud whoop. "Intense just like your old man, and it's gonna help us win the competition!"

"What do you mean 'intense just like your old man'?" Norm pouted.

"Aw, come on, boss. It's a good thing. You're obsessed with ingredients, and Jackal seems to be following in your footsteps," Rusty said.

I guess I am, Jack thought as his feet tapped enthusiastically against his stool.

Marvelous Jackson

"Let's get a batch of nuggies marinating right now. We can keep them in the fridge overnight and try out the new batter tomorrow," Norm said. "The competition is a week from Sunday, so we've got just enough time to work out the kinks and get everything perfect."

Rusty held his spatula in the air. "Go, team."

Dusty high-fived Rusty's spatula with a wire whisk.

Meanwhile, Norm opened a jar of pickles and stuck his nose in. "Smell that dill . . . and ginger . . . and bay leaf."

And Jack sat on his stool, taking in the whole scene, thankful that he was no longer hiding in a bathroom stall at the library.

He was exactly where he needed to be.

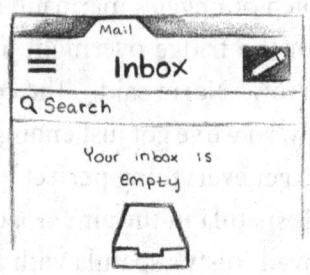

Twenty-Four
Greatness Takes Time

Over the weekend, Jack checked his email repeatedly for any messages from *MMKBC*, but his inbox remained maddeningly empty. He dug the heels of his hands into his eye sockets and wanted to scream.

You applied on a whim at the very last minute, he reminded himself. *It's not like you were preparing your whole life to be on a baking show. You have to get over it.*

The only thing that made him feel better was hearing from Norm that the latest batch of nuggies—made with pickle juice and confectioners' sugar—was delicious.

"Does that mean the recipe is finalized?" Jack asked him.

"Darn tootin'. Thanks to you."

. . .

Marvelous Jackson

By Monday morning, Jack was sick of opening his email and feeling nothing but disappointment. So as he biked to Evergreen, he tried to give himself a pep talk.

You don't have to be on TV to prove yourself. You just need to bake. It's your hobby, after all. It has to be enough.

"Hey, would you guys give me a baking project?" he asked Carlos and Pogo when he got to school.

"What do you mean? Don't you use cookbooks?" Pogo said.

"Yes, but I want to start taking special requests, to keep me challenged. I don't want to fall into a rut. I need to keep learning new things," Jack said. *And then I won't have time to think about* MMKBC.

"How about a Creamy Kalamazoo Cake?" Carlos suggested.

"OK," Jack said.

"What about me? Don't I get a special request, too?" Pogo whined.

"Next time," Jack said.

"Can I get my cake tonight, *niño*?"

"*Tonight?* Are you kidding? I have to buy ingredients at the store and then teach myself how to make one. You'll just have to be patient." Jack scoffed. "Greatness takes time."

"But it's just layers of yellow cake, and creamy filling, and fudge icing. It shouldn't be that hard," Carlos said, sticking out his bottom lip.

"Speak for yourself," Jack retorted.

When he got home, he found a recipe for **Creamy Kalamazoo Cake** in his mom's cookbook. The directions didn't look easy, but they didn't look impossible, either. Now that he had more baking experience, he could at least give it a try.

Twenty-Five
Creamy Kalamazoo Cake

After school on Tuesday, Jack biked to the supermarket to buy ingredients.

After school on Wednesday, he watched videos of people making Creamy Kalamazoo Cake, and he took notes as if he were in Miss Kibble's English class.

After school on Thursday, he baked.

After school on Friday, Jack told Carlos the cake was ready to be picked up, and at five o'clock on the dot, the doorbell of his cottage rang.

Carefully, Jack opened the door, and Carlos gaped at the Creamy Kalamazoo Cake. "You made that all by yourself?"

Jack handed it over to Carlos like it was an infant. "Yep."

"I didn't think you could do it."

"Thanks for the vote of confidence." Jack punched Carlos in the arm, but not too hard, because he didn't want him to drop the cake—or the nice white platter it was on.

"Sorry. What I mean is that I told you how easy it was to make a Creamy Kalamazoo Cake, but I had no idea what I was talking about. My mom yelled at me and said they're super tricky. But you did it." Carlos thrust some money at Jack. "That's from her. We're going to my aunt's house for lunch tomorrow, and we're planning to take the cake with us. My mom says thanks."

"I didn't do it for money," Jack said, even as he relished tucking the twenty dollars into his pocket.

"I know, but you saved her a lot of time."

Carlos's mom waved from the car, and Jack waved back. "Keep it refrigerated," he instructed Carlos. "And bring back the platter when you're done."

"I will, *niño*."

Jack didn't know what was most remarkable—that he'd baked something difficult, that he'd just made twenty bucks off it, or that his mom's beautiful platter was in use again.

Twenty-Six
In a Voice as Rich as Chocolate

On Saturday, Jack didn't sleep late. He woke up early, even before Norm.

He had dreamed about his mom all night. She'd been in the kitchen, with her ginger hair tied back and little flecks of flour on her cheeks. She was baking Caramel Apple Spice Knots, which she'd always made this time of year, when autumn was leaning into winter.

Jack wasn't sure how somebody could actually smell something in a dream, but when his eyes flicked open, he was convinced there was a batch of Caramel Apple Spice Knots right there in his bedroom. That wasn't the case, but now he knew how he wanted to spend his day.

Thanks for the idea, Mom.

In his mind, she winked one of her gray eyes at him.

He padded to the kitchen and began gathering his ingredients.

When his phone rang a little while later, Jack didn't recognize the number. He wiped cookie dough off his hands and debated whether to pick up. He was sure it was just a telemarketer, but curiosity got the best of him.

"Hello?" he answered.

"Is this Jackson Jefferson Wilson?" the caller asked in a voice as rich as chocolate.

In a voice that sounds exactly like Shane O'Shaughnessy's.

"Um, yes?" Jack's knees felt wobbly, as if all the bones had just slid out. He fell into a kitchen chair as he tried to make sense of why Shane O'Shaughnessy was on the line. He'd expected to receive an impersonal email from *MMKBC* saying something like *Sorry, you're not invited to Chicago. Keep dreaming, kid.* A phone call made no sense.

"This is Shane O'Shaughnessy from *The Marvelous Midwest Kids Baking Championship*, and you've been selected by our esteemed panel of judges to audition in person for our next season!"

Jack stood up so fast, he knocked his carton of eggs right off the table. They landed on the floor with a crack, and yolks and whites began oozing from the cardboard container.

"Jackson? Are you there?" Shane O'Shaughnessy said. "Hellooo?"

Marvelous Jackson

"I'm here. I guess I'm in . . . shock." Jack's mouth felt sticky. "I wanted this so bad, and I'm just . . . surprised. And happy."

Shane O'Shaughnessy laughed. "I can imagine it's not often you receive a call from a celebrity host, inviting you to try out for a big-hearted, world-famous, award-winning television show."

"That's correct." Jack smiled so big, tears sprang to his eyes.

"Allow me to be the first to applaud you on a terrific application. You were angsty, vulnerable, original, and honest. We loved your vibe, Jackson."

Jack didn't know what angsty meant, but Shane O'Shaughnessy went on before he could ask.

"We think you would bring a depth and moodiness to the competition that we haven't seen before. We think a lot of young people would be able to relate to you and your baking journey, and we like that you're eager to keep learning and practicing."

"Oh," Jack said.

"Sometimes we have kids on the show who've been baking *forever* and think they know *everything*. They can be a bit exasperating, but don't tell a soul that you heard that from me."

Jack promised he wouldn't.

"Also, you've got an impressive head of hair, which we think would look fantastic on camera."

Jack ran his hands through his thicket of bangs. "Thanks."

"Auditions are at our studio in Chicago one week from tomorrow. Sunday morning. Bright and early. Nine o'clock."

"Wait, *what*?" Jack stepped over the broken eggs and started pacing the kitchen. *That's the same day as the nuggie contest.*

"Is there a problem, Jackson?"

Jack covered his face with his hands. "Um, well," he finally said. "Yes. There's a problem."

"What's the matter?"

"I, well . . . my dad has something going on at the same time, and I promised I would be there to help him."

"Hmm," Shane O'Shaughnessy said, and Jack could hear him literally scratching his head. "Perhaps you and your dad could figure out an alternate plan? I'd hate to think of your spot going to someone else."

Jack stared in misery at his bowl of Caramel Apple Spice dough on the counter. To have worked so hard to secure an audition only to end up declining the offer made him feel as empty as a pie with no filling. "It's really important . . ."

After a pause, Shane O'Shaughnessy said, "I'll tell you what. I'll email you a permission slip for your audition, and I'll keep my fingers crossed that you and your dad can come up with a solution. After all, more than a *thousand* kids applied for our new season, and only thirty-six of them have been invited to Chicago."

Jack couldn't believe he'd made it into such an elite group.

"From those thirty-six kids, twelve will be offered a spot on the show."

Jack swallowed. Knowing the math only made the whole situation more excruciating. His heart felt as demolished as the eggshells at his feet.

"The signed permission slip is due by five o'clock today, so be in touch right away if you don't think it's going to work out," Shane O'Shaughnessy said.

Jack agreed, and they said goodbye.

He wrapped his arms around himself.

I got an audition! I got an audition! I got an audition!

But why did it have to be at the same time as the nuggie competition?

Jack wanted to weep, laugh, and shout all at once, but Norm was sleeping, so he couldn't make a fuss. He logged into his email, and sure enough, the *MMKBC* permission slip was already in his inbox—proof that his phone call with Shane O'Shaughnessy hadn't been a figment of his wildest imagination.

Jack printed out the permission slip and wondered how to approach Norm about the audition. He needed his dad to be in a good mood when he brought it up, but beyond that, he wasn't sure how to handle the situation, or what to expect. He had no idea if Norm would be furious, disappointed, ecstatic, or something else entirely.

He folded the permission slip and slid it into his back pocket. It would be safe there, until he figured out what to do next.

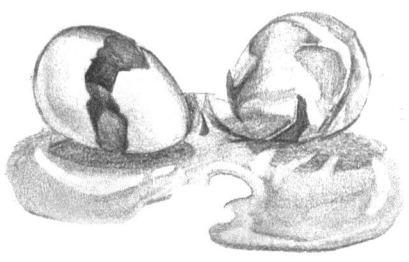

Twenty-Seven
Today is Not the Day

Jack cleaned up his eggy mess and biked to the supermarket to buy another dozen. As he pedaled across Alwyn, he became certain that he could have a good talk with Norm about his *MMKBC* dilemma. He couldn't predict what his dad would say, but he felt like they'd come a long way over the last few weeks—enough to listen to each other and remain calm.

When Jack got home, he was dismayed to find that Norm had already left for Dutch's. A note was on the counter: *Had to go to work early to get a rack of ribs in the oven. See you later, buddy.*

Jack put his eggs in the fridge and went outside, where he climbed back on his bike. He would follow his dad all around town if he had to.

At Dutch's, Dusty was grating a gigantic block of

cheese. "What're you doing here so early on a Saturday, Jacky?"

Jack sat down on a stool and grabbed a handful of cherry tomatoes from a bowl on the counter. "Just looking for my dad. I need to talk to him."

"He's having a meeting with our soda salesman in the dining room, so you might have to wait a little while. Our root beer vendor is going out of business, so we need to find a new one, which apparently is a very high-stress situation. It's been a rough day so far." Dusty stopped shredding his cheddar and looked at Jack. "Everything OK with you?"

"Yes and no . . ." Jack came clean with Dusty about how he'd applied for *MMKBC* and had just received a phone call from Shane O'Shaughnessy.

Dusty's mouth fell open. "Shane O'Shaughnessy called you?"

Jack nodded.

A second later, Rusty pushed through the swinging door. He was working front of house, which meant he wasn't wearing his usual studded jewelry. Instead, he had on a plain black t-shirt and dark jeans, and his hair was slicked into a topknot. He clapped Jack on the back. "What's up, Jackal?"

Jack nearly choked on his tomato.

"Rusty, get a load of this. Our Jacky got invited to audition in Chicago for a baking show! Like a real one—on television and everything," Dusty said.

Marvelous Jackson

"What're you talking about, man?" Rusty clapped Jack's back a second time.

Jack went through the details again. "I'm still learning how to bake, but I guess *MMKBC* likes my vibe," he added. "They don't want all their contestants to be experienced and perfect."

"Who needs perfection anyway? It's overrated." Rusty gave Jack a lopsided smile.

"Your old man's gonna be so proud of you," Dusty said.

Jack shook his head miserably. "No, no. There's a huge problem."

"How can there be a *problem*? You were chosen out of a thousand kids to audition!" Dusty exclaimed.

Jack slouched on his stool. "The audition is a week from tomorrow. The same day as the nuggie competition."

Dusty and Rusty groaned.

Jack pulled the permission slip from his pocket and smoothed it out on the counter. "I promised my dad I would help you guys . . . which means I can't audition for *MMKBC*."

"Wait a minute, Jackal. You gotta talk to your pops. I mean, you've been crucial to our nuggie endeavors so far, but your audition is way more important," Rusty said.

"You think?"

"Absolutely," Dusty insisted. "Talk to the boss and

see what he says. We've sure loved having your help, but I think we'll be A-OK if you're not at the nuggie competition."

Rusty pointed to the permission slip. "Whaddya got there?"

"My permission slip, which is due by five o'clock today. So if I *were* going to audition, I would need to get it signed *right now*." Jack sighed. "But even if my dad miraculously tells me that I can go, who's going to drive me to Chicago?"

Norm banged through the swinging door. "The new root beer prices the soda guy gave me are ridiculous!" He smacked his hand against the metal counter, sending a tinny echo through the kitchen. "And we just ran out of straws!"

Ugh, Jack thought.

Norm's hair was rumpled, and it looked as though he hadn't showered or slept very well.

Instinctively, Jack knew it wasn't the right moment to bring up *MMKBC*. He needed to find another time when Norm wasn't falling apart—but it needed to be very soon. With a sinking feeling, he folded his permission slip into a square, as if it were origami.

"Listen, boss," Dusty said. "We can look into other options for root beer, and as for the straws, Rusty and I will—"

But Norm didn't appear to be listening because he'd just registered Jack's presence. "What're you doing here, buddy?"

"Um, I just stopped by for . . ." Jack faltered.

Marvelous Jackson

"For some cherry tomatoes," Rusty said, pushing the bowl closer to Jack. "He's a growing kid, and he's hungry."

Norm's eyebrows pushed together. "OK. Sure."

"Eat up, buttercup." Rusty winked at Jack.

Jack pushed another cherry tomato in his mouth. "I could bike to the supermarket and buy some straws, if that would help," he told Norm.

"Sure thing. That would be great. Paper, not plastic. Save the environment."

Jack nodded.

Norm turned back toward the dining room. "Now, if you fellas will excuse me, I have some Shirley Temples to make."

As Norm turned back to the swinging door, Rusty tugged the permission slip from Jack's hand and unfolded it. "Hey, wait. Can you sign this first? It's for the nuggie competition. It's a form that says our recipe is original." Rusty shoved the permission slip at Norm, along with a pen that had been jammed in his bun.

"Darn tootin' our recipe is *original*. With credit going to Chef Kelly Clinton of Connecticut for the addition of pickle juice and confectioners' sugar, of course." Norm signed the form without reading a word.

Norm hurried off, and Rusty handed the permission slip back to Jack. "This'll buy you a little time, Jackal, so you can talk to your pops when he's not so stressed out."

"But when is Norm *not* stressed out?" Jack said.

No one in the kitchen had an answer for that.

Twenty-Eight
From Bad to Worse

After buying an industrial-size box of straws at the supermarket and delivering it to Dutch's, Jack returned to the cottage. His phone rang as he pulled off his tennis shoes. Why was Norm calling? They'd just seen each other. There was no way he'd already run out of straws again.

"That kid you slugged in the hallway at school. Or tripped. Or pushed. Or *whatever* you did," Norm spat out.

"Benny?" Jack said.

"Yeah, Benny. His parents just called me to discuss the bill from his dentist. Were you aware that it was five hundred dollars? Did you know they expected us to pay it?"

Jack grimaced. Norm's day had just gone from bad to worse, and it was all because of him. "Benny sort of mentioned it a while ago, but he never said for sure . . ."

Marvelous Jackson

"Why didn't you tell me?" Norm yelled.

"I don't know. It wasn't definite . . . and you've been busy with nuggies and stuff."

"I wish you would've been upfront from the start, so I didn't sound like such a dolt on the phone. We're getting clobbered with the lunch crowd right now, and I could barely focus on what Benny's parents were saying!"

Jack listened to the clash and clang of Dutch's as his dad breathed raggedly. "I'm really sorry," he said.

"We'll discuss this tomorrow. And don't *ever* trip or push anyone again. Do you understand?"

"Yes, obviously. I haven't done anything like that in—"

The line went dead before he could finish.

Jack crumpled to the living room floor, not far from the spot where he'd always played *Candy Smash*.

What do I do now?

He and Norm needed to talk—that much was clear. They needed to talk about his *MMKBC* audition and Benny's tooth and the five hundred dollars. But Jack was running out of time. *If I wait for Norm to cheer up, it'll be too late for me to send my permission slip to Shane O'Shaughnessy.*

As his face smooshed further into the wooly nap of the carpet, Jack made a decision. He wasn't sure if it was the right one, because it wasn't completely honest, but he couldn't bear to miss out on the opportunity that had been given to him.

He wanted to turn in his permission slip, just to be safe, even if it meant telling Shane O'Shaughnessy later that he couldn't make it to Chicago.

Jack pulled out his phone.

And a minute later, after snapping a photograph of his signed permission slip, he used his quivering thumb to press *SEND*.

Twenty-Nine
Whooshy

Jack stood in front of the stove the next morning, wondering what kind of eggs to make for Norm. Fried? Poached? Sunny-side-up? He decided on scrambled.

His mom's cookbook had a recipe for scrambled eggs, but heavy cream was listed as an ingredient, and Jack knew there was none in the fridge. He crossed his fingers and hoped regular milk would work.

The kitchen already smelled delicious from the Caramel Apple Spice Knots he'd finally gotten around to baking. His goal was for Norm to wake up to a pleasing aroma in the cottage, which would hopefully set the stage for a good conversation. He'd planned out everything he wanted to say.

The only thing missing was coffee. He wished he knew how to use the espresso machine, because his dad didn't resemble a human being until he'd guzzled some caffeine, but Jack had no clue which buttons to press.

Norm shuffled downstairs wearing pajama pants and a t-shirt that said *I BRAKE FOR BRATWURST* across the front. He rubbed his eyes and grumbled, "Man, it smells good in here. Happy Sunday."

Jack smiled to himself as he stirred the eggs. His plan was off to a good start.

Norm brewed an espresso and slumped into a kitchen chair. A few minutes later, when Jack presented him with a plate of eggs and cookies, Norm finally spoke. "What did I do to deserve all this?"

"Nothing. I just need to talk to you."

Norm sipped his mug of foamy brown liquid. "Talking is good. We should've been doing more of it over the last four hundred and . . ." Norm wrinkled his forehead, and Jack realized *he'd* been tallying the days, too. And, just like Jack, Norm had apparently lost count.

"Buddy, I'm real sorry," Norm went on.

Jack tilted his head. He hadn't known what to expect, but it certainly wasn't an apology. "Sorry for what?"

"For being tired and crabby all the time. For working at Dutch's too much. Honestly, I don't know if I can keep going at this speed. At least hunting season is winding down, and there's only one week left until the nuggie competition. Once that's over, I'll have more free time."

Marvelous Jackson

Jack seriously doubted that, because Norm hadn't had any free time for as long as he could remember, but he merely nodded. "Speaking of the nuggie competition..."

Norm shoveled some scrambled eggs into his mouth. "Fluffy," he murmured. "Nice touch of Tabasco. No cream?"

"No cream. Just milk," Jack confirmed. "So, something's come up next Sunday."

Norm stopped chewing. "Nuggie competition day? What do you mean?"

Jack sat down next to Norm and took a deep breath. He explained how he had applied for *MMKBC*, and how he'd been invited to Chicago to audition. He described Shane O'Shaughnessy's phone call and how it had been the most incredible thing to ever happen to him.

Norm's expression was unreadable. "But couldn't you push off your audition until next year? Head to Chicago when things are a little less crazy around here?"

"I'll be too old. This is my only chance."

"But you said you were going to help with the nuggies."

"I know, I know—and I *want* to help with them... if the nuggie competition were on a different day." Jack's stomach began to churn. A small part of him had believed Norm would let him off the hook, but that didn't seem likely now. "The top prize for *MMKBC* is twenty thousand dollars," he added in a last-ditch effort.

Norm's fork clattered to his plate. "Really?"

Jack nodded. "There's no guarantee that I would win—or make it onto the show in the first place—but if I did, I'd have the money to pay for Benny's broken tooth. *And* buy Dutch's a lifetime supply of root beer. *And* get you guys a new salad bar, and carpeting, and video games."

And purchase more baking supplies for the cottage! he thought, picturing all the cool things he'd seen on *MMKBC*, like springform pans, baking mats, and batter dispensers.

"Buddy..."

"I've been thinking about a lot of things, Dad. I've decided that if I can't be a contestant on *MMKBC*, then I'll work for you at Dutch's. It'd be cool to get paid for something I'm good at." Jack thought of the twenty dollars Carlos's mom had given him for the Creamy Kalamazoo Cake and the satisfaction it had brought. "Cooking isn't baking, but it's close enough. And being at Dutch's isn't so bad."

"But I didn't think you wanted to smell like a restaurant every day, or get into debates about ingredients." Norm laid his palms flat against the table. "Aren't I too *intense* for you?"

Jack frowned. "I'm sorry for saying those things and hurting your feelings. I've come a long way since then." He meant it, but at the same time, he could see his entire plan going up in flames. He wanted to sob.

But then Norm leaned back in his chair and laughed, and Jack could see he was teasing.

Marvelous Jackson

Maybe there was still hope!

"I'm sorry if I came on too strong about Benny's tooth," Norm said. "I can afford the five hundred dollars, so please don't worry about that. I was just angry that you'd gotten into a scrape with that kid in the first place, but Lord knows I did some stupid things when I was young, too." Norm got a funny look on his face.

"Like what?" Jack asked, perhaps too eagerly.

"We're not talking about *me*, we're talking about *you*. Not only have you turned things around at school and at home, but you just got an audition for the most famous baking show in the country!" Norm punched the air with a fist.

Jack grinned. He could feel it: little by little, Norm was coming around to *MMKBC*.

"I'm real proud of you, buddy, and I know your mom would be, too. There's no question about it. You have to go to your audition."

"Really?" Jack felt whooshy, as if his body temperature had just gone up a few degrees. He could feel his heartbeat in his ears.

"Yep, and I'm not just saying that because of the cash prize, even though it's a dandy. I mean, look at how this hobby of yours has changed your life! You're not getting in trouble anymore, and it seems like the rain cloud that was always hanging over your head has disappeared."

"Oh," Jack said. He hadn't noticed the rain cloud, but he was glad it was gone.

"But here's the rub, buddy. I can't be in two places at once. I would love to take you to Chicago, but I can't abandon Dutch's so close to the competition. We've been preparing for a long time."

"I know," Jack said. "What if I got a ride with somebody else?"

"Who on earth would take you all the way to Chicago and back? It's a long drive, especially this time of year when the weather's so fickle. Winter's coming."

Jack's mind raced. So many people had helped him over the past month, but this would be the biggest favor yet. He knew it was a lot to ask.

"Actually . . ." Norm drummed his fingers against his jaw. "Lemme talk to Dusty."

"Dusty? He can't drive me. He has to work at the nuggie competition."

"He has a sister named Annabelle who goes to Chicago a lot. She owns Hug in a Mug, the café on Juniper Street, and she gets all her coffee beans from a distributor in Bucktown. Dusty says they're amazing. They're fair trade from Colombia, with a bold fragrance and a hint of sweetness and—"

"Could you talk to him?" Jack interrupted. "Like today?"

"I'll see what I can do. We're hosting a big meat raffle later, so it's gonna be—"

Marvelous Jackson

"Crazy," Jack interjected, because it was *always* crazy at Dutch's.

"Yes, it'll be nuts, but I'll do my best." Norm ruffled Jack's hair, just like he'd done when Jack was little. "You deserve it."

Jack closed his eyes and wished the moment would never end.

Thirty
Bright and Early, One Week from Tomorrow

Jack was right. It was always crazy at Dutch's, but his phone rang anyway, later that afternoon. He saw Dusty's number on the screen and answered as fast as he could.

"Boss told me it's a green light for you to audition, which is terrific news, Jacky!" Dusty said. "I'm glad he's warming up to the whole baking thing. Now we gotta find you some transportation, right?"

Jack felt a little breathless. "Yep."

"I'm trying to reach my sister as we speak, but she's a bridesmaid in a wedding in Minneapolis, so she's occupied at the present moment."

Jack's shoulders fell. How long would it take for Annabelle to get back to Dusty?

Marvelous Jackson

"What time do you have to be in Chicago for your audition?"

"Bright and early," Jack said, quoting Shane O'Shaughnessy. "Nine o'clock. Next Sunday."

There was a long, low whistle in the background that sounded an awful lot like Rusty.

"Is that Rusty?" Jack asked.

"Of course," Dusty said. "He's in the storage closet with me."

"Um, why are you guys in the storage closet?"

"Because it's super loud out there—you know, with the meat raffle and everything."

"Oh, right." Jack smiled. *Dusty and Rusty are squished together in a storage closet during a meat raffle just so they can help me.*

"Man, it's like a six-hour drive from Alwyn to Chicago!" Rusty hollered.

"Lucky for us, Annabelle is a morning person," Dusty said. "Like a middle-of-the-night morning person. If she can drive you, Jacky, you'll have to leave Alwyn by three a.m. to get to Chicago in time."

There was a thump, and Rusty moaned. "Aw, jeez, you just stepped on my toe, Dusty."

"We gotta go, Jacky. Your old man is yelling for us," Dusty said.

Sure enough, Jack heard Norm shouting something about relish trays and bacon-wrapped tenderloins.

"I must be claustrophobic, because I'm sweating like a bank robber in church," Rusty said.

"As soon as I hear from Annabelle, I'll let you know," Dusty said to Jack and clicked off.

Jack tried to slow his racing pulse. He stared out the window of the cottage into what his mom had referred to as the gloaming. It always took him by surprise, how dark the afternoons were this time of year. He was sure they contained every shade of purple.

If Annabelle can drive me to Chicago, then I'll be at the MMKBC studio exactly one week from right now.

His hands began to sweat.

I'll have to bake in front of people I've never met before, and answer all their questions, and act like I know what I'm doing.

He wiped his palms on his jeans. It was time to tell his friends.

Thirty-One
Brand-New Group Text

Jack didn't know which friend to text first. Theo? Carlos? Pogo? Clare?

He threw his hands in the air and decided to create a brand-new group text with everybody on it, even Lola, although he wasn't positive that she'd stopped hating him yet.

In a rush, and with a number of typos that would've made Miss Kibble wince, he sent his friends a lengthy, bumbling message. His nervous energy made it hard to explain everything in an organized way, but he figured the only detail that mattered was that Shane O'Shaughnessy had called to offer him an audition spot for *MMKBC*.

Clare and Theo freaked out. *Congratulations!* they texted back, along with emojis of cakes, cookies, balloons, and clapping hands.

Lola texted him a winky face. *You're obsessed! I knew it!*

Pogo asked if the whole thing was a joke, and Carlos said no way, because Jack's Creamy Kalamazoo Cake had been a hit at his aunt's house. *He's got what it takes. He's going to get picked to be on the show, and then he'll be F A M O U S.*

Everybody wanted to know if Shane O'Shaughnessy was as nice on the phone as he seemed on the show.

Yep, Jack replied.

Will you be ready for your audition? they asked him.

Jack sighed. The question that weighed most heavily on him was *Will Annabelle be able to drive me?*

His friends kept going.

Are you nervous?

Do you need to practice?

How are you going to prepare?

And Jack replied, truthfully, *I don't know. Keep on baking by myself, I guess.*

By yourself? everyone texted. *THAT'S NO FUN.*

...

That evening, the doorbell rang.

Jack had barely turned the doorknob when Theo, Carlos, Pogo, and Lola barged in like a pack of wild animals. He stepped back as they streamed into his cottage. "What's going on?" he yelled, alarmed.

"We're here to help you get ready for your audition!" Theo replied.

"We're giving you a baking boot camp," Carlos said.

Jack gaped at them.

"Theo organized this whole thing, in case you're wondering." Playfully, Lola pinched her brother's cheek. "He thought it'd be fun for us all to get together and help a baker in need."

Indeed, Jack was amazed that Theo, Carlos, Pogo, and Lola were in the same place at the same time. That had never happened before.

"We can't stand to see you go to Chicago so *woefully* ill prepared," Lola added.

"Um, thanks?" Jack said, and everybody laughed.

"By the way, dude, this challenge is all mine." Pogo elbowed Jack. "You owe me, remember?"

Jack nodded.

"Less chatting, more baking," Theo said, and started down the hallway.

As everybody followed him, Lola stuck her phone up to Jack's face, and he saw that Clare was on the screen.

"I wanted to be part of baking boot camp, too," she said.

"Oh." He couldn't get any other words out. *All* his friends had showed up for him, even the one who was hundreds of miles away. Gratitude filled his chest cavity, and his hoodie suddenly felt too warm. "Thanks," he managed to say.

Lola took Jack's hand and pulled him to the kitchen, where everyone was unpacking grocery bags. "My mom took us to the supermarket, and we got a few things."

"I'm guessing she went overboard, as usual?"

"You know it, Jackers."

Jackers? That was a new one. He grinned.

Theo grabbed one of Jack's mom's old aprons and threw it at him. "Put that on, because your time starts soon."

Jack yanked off his hoodie and tied the apron over his t-shirt. He made a point of ignoring Carlos and Pogo, who snickered at the faded flowers and frilly lace.

"Get out all your mixing bowls and measuring spoons," Lola said.

"Are you going to tell me what I'm supposed to be baking?" Jack asked.

"Of course," Pogo said. "You're supposed to be baking—"

"Drumroll, please," Carlos interjected, and everyone pounded their hands on the kitchen table.

"—two dozen Scotchie Bites."

"Am I supposed to know what Scotchie Bites are?" Jack asked.

"Duh, *yes*. My favorite cookie in the world." Pogo smacked his lips.

"But I don't have a recipe for them."

"You won't be able to use any recipes when you're at

the *MMKBC* studio," Theo reminded him.

"It's OK if you don't know how to make Scotchie Bites," Clare said from Chicago. "You've baked other stuff, so you can improvise."

Jack knew Theo and Clare were right, but he was caught in a vise grip of panic. Suddenly, what he *didn't* know felt so much bigger than what he *did*.

"Jack." Theo grabbed him by the shoulders. "You can do this. You know how to make cookies. Don't freak out."

Jack reviewed the recipes that were lodged in his brain. Unfortunately, there weren't many to choose from. "Sugar Dumplings," he said.

"Yes!" Theo exclaimed. "Use Sugar Dumplings as your starting point. Begin with the basics, and by the end, you'll have Scotchie Bites."

Pogo shoved a bag of butterscotch chips at him and shouted, "Your time starts right now!"

Just like Ellie, Jack closed his eyes and inhaled deeply. He felt oxygen breeze through all the circuits in his body.

"What's he doing?" Pogo whispered.

"Isn't he supposed to be running around and yelling like they do on those cooking shows?" Carlos whispered back.

"Just give him a minute," Theo said.

Jack tuned everybody out as he exhaled. He thought about the ingredients he would need and each step he'd have to take. He pieced together a plan, which unfurled before him like an orderly path. He would follow it, step by step. He would remember everything he'd learned from watching *MMKBC* and reading cookbook after cookbook at the library.

Manage your time.
Measure carefully.
Follow the rules.
Be creative.
Stay calm.
Be nice.

Jack opened his eyes and made a loop through the kitchen, pulling items from the fridge, the pantry, and the stash of groceries Marisa had bought.

"Oats?" Pogo protested when he saw the container in Jack's hand. "My mom's Scotchie Bites don't have *oats* in them."

"His Scotchie Bites aren't your mama's Scotchie Bites." Carlos swatted Pogo's head. "In fact, they're probably gonna be better. No disrespect to your mama, though."

Pogo swatted Carlos back.

If I can ignore them, I can deal with a television camera pointing in my face, Jack thought.

Meanwhile, his friends made a show of getting comfortable.

Pogo put his feet up on the table, and Lola knocked them off. "Manners!" she hissed.

Theo begged Clare to put her little dog, Roger, on the screen. Theo cooed at him, and Roger yipped in response.

Carlos began to comment on every little thing Jack did, just like an overeager sportscaster. "In a superhuman feat of power and endurance, Jackson Jefferson Wilson breaks an egg into a medium-size bowl," he said, leaning into a pretend microphone.

Jack cracked another egg.

"Ope! I think he got some shell in that one," Carlos announced.

Carlos was right about the shell, and Jack lost a few precious minutes scooping out the tiny white fragments. *Don't get rattled*, he told himself.

A few minutes later, he messed up again when he dumped flour in the mixing bowl too fast. It puffed up into his face, making him sneeze three times.

"Rookie mistake," Carlos said into his microphone.

"Keep going," Theo implored him.

Jack got tripped up once more when it was time to add baking powder—or was it baking soda? His mind had gone blank.

He knew that baking powder and baking soda both gave baked goods their fluffiness, but they worked differently—he just couldn't remember *how*. So he added a little bit of each and hoped for the best.

Seconds before the kitchen timer was set to beep, Jack slid the last of his two dozen Scotchie Bites onto the cooling rack.

"It hasn't been a flawless performance, folks, but Jackson Jefferson Wilson's cookies smell outstanding," Carlos declared. "I think we have a winner."

Jack wiped his hands on his mom's apron. "You should probably try one before you say that."

"*Exactly*," Pogo said. "Does that mean we can eat them now?"

"No. They need to cool first. Don't you know anything about baking?" Lola said.

Pogo shrugged.

Everyone pitched in to clean up the kitchen, and as soon as they were finished, Pogo insisted that the Scotchie Bites were cool enough to be eaten. Jack placed the cookies on his mom's daffodil-yellow platter and set it on the table.

The Scotchie Bites began to disappear, and the only sound was of everyone's chewing.

Jack tapped his foot. "So, what do you think?" he finally said. "You have to give me a critique."

"In that case," Pogo said, stretching back in his chair, "I think the cookies need more butterscotch."

"No way," Lola said. "'To loathe the taste of sweetness, whereof little more than a little is by much too much.'"

Pogo grunted. "What does *that* mean?"

"*Romeo and Juliet*. Don't you ever read Shakespeare?"

Pogo gave her a pointed look. "No."

"She means just because you *can* doesn't mean you *should*. You have to go easy with things like butterscotch.

Marvelous Jackson

Restraint is everything," Jack said.

"That sounds like something my mom would say," Lola murmured.

"Some of your Scotchie Bites are thick and chewy, but the other ones are too thin," Carlos told him.

"You have to make sure all your cookies are the same size," Theo reminded Jack. "If your scoops of dough are equal, they'll bake uniformly."

Jack nodded. He stood tall and straight, just like the *MMKBC* contestants did when they were being judged.

"I admit that your cookies taste pretty good, but dude, we need to talk about the oats. *Why? Why* did you add them?" Pogo clasped his hands together as if begging for mercy.

"I thought they would enhance the texture and flavor." Jack had learned the word "enhance" from Ellie. "They also make the Scotchie Bites a little healthier."

"Who wants *healthy* when eating cookies?" Pogo said.

Everyone dissolved into giggles.

As they polished off the platter, leaving no crumb behind, Jack reviewed the challenge. He'd made some mistakes, but he'd fixed them all. He'd answered his friends' questions and taken their feedback to heart. It had been nerve-wracking to bake in front of other people, whose eyes were glued to his every move, but he'd done it.

He wondered if this was how it felt to be a boxer—being pummeled to the ground one minute and hopping

back up the next. He had a new respect for Abby.
Get ready, he told himself. *This is just the beginning.*

Thirty-Two
No Oats, I Promise

Jack texted Dusty first thing Monday to see if he'd heard anything from Annabelle. Dusty wrote back that she was still in Minneapolis with her friends.

"How long does a stupid wedding take, anyway?" Jack wanted to throw his phone across his bedroom.

She'll be in touch with you as soon as she can, Dusty said.

Jack hoped he was right.

When he got to Evergreen, he was accosted by Carlos. "Report to Pogo's house immediately after school today."

"For what?"

"For one more baking boot camp. It's the only night this week that all of us are free, and we thought you could use a little more practice."

Pogo, who'd snuck up behind Jack, yelled in his ear, "But I swear, dude, no oats this time. Promise?"

"I don't even know what I'll be making yet," Jack protested. "But fine—no oats. I promise."

...

"Attention, attention!" Pogo called out, attempting to silence his noisy kitchen. "Welcome to day two of baking boot camp."

Everyone clapped.

"Your challenge today is to bake a pan of brownies," he told Jack.

"Just a pan of brownies?" Jack narrowed his eyes. "Do I have to use any special ingredients?"

"Nope," Pogo answered.

"Are any ingredients off-limits?"

"Aside from oats, you mean?" Pogo said.

"Nothing's off-limits," Theo confirmed.

"This seems a little . . . easy. What's the twist?" Jack asked.

"You can only use one hand!" everybody said at once.

"Oh," Jack replied. He hadn't expected that.

Carlos tied Jack's left arm behind his back with a winter scarf that belonged to Pogo's little sister. "There, that should work."

"At least I'm right-handed," Jack quipped.

Marvelous Jackson

"Shane O'Shaughnessy always gives the contestants at least one challenge like this during the season," Lola said. "If it's not having your arm tied up, it's having your eyes covered with a blindfold, or your nose plugged with a clothespin. You have to be ready for anything."

Jack knew she was right.

He was able to mix, stir, and pour all right, but when he pulled his pan of brownies out of the oven and slid a knife through them, he could see they were a mess. *How did this happen?*

"I'm not sure they're cooked all the way through," Theo said.

"They're extremely . . . walnutty." Lola grimaced.

"Where's all the chocolate?" Carlos asked. "You skimped on the chips."

Pogo scrunched up his nose and pushed the pan away without a word.

"It's hard to keep everything straight when I'm not using a cookbook," Jack said.

"Don't let it mess with your head, Prez!" Clare exclaimed from Lola's phone.

"*Prez?*" Carlos said, and made a kissy face.

Jack couldn't understand why he seemed to be getting worse at baking, not better.

His phone buzzed, so he fished it out of his pocket with his free hand.

Hi, Jackson, the message said. *This is Annabelle. My brother said you needed some help.*

Jack gasped, and everyone turned to look at him. "Hold on, I need a minute," he said. "Can you untie my arm?"

Carlos pulled off the scarf, and Jack ducked into the hallway.

Annabelle

> I have to drive to Chicago this weekend to pick up coffee beans for my shop. I could go on Sunday and take you to your audition. Would that work?

Jack

> Yes!

He couldn't type the word fast enough.

Annabelle

> Dusty told me you need to be downtown by 9, so we'll leave super early—like the middle of the night. Can you be ready by 3 a.m.?

Marvelous Jackson

Jack

Annabelle

Ha, I guess we won't hit any traffic that time of day!

Jack

Annabelle

Do you think I'll be able to catch a glimpse of THE Shane O'Shaughnessy when I drop you off at the studio? Gosh, I love that guy.

Jack leaned against the wall to steady himself. How amazing would it be to meet Shane O'Shaughnessy? And Vicky Willow? And Archie Gomez?

"Holy cow," he breathed. Anything was possible.

Annabelle

I'll pack us a carnic.

Jack

What's that?

Annabelle

A picnic for the car.

> **Jack**
> Great, I'll bake us something for dessert

> **Annabelle**
> Thanks. I'm no good at baking. See you Sunday!

Jack ran back into the kitchen, shrieking, "I'm going to Chicago!"

"Duh," Pogo said. "We already knew that."

"No. I mean I'm *really* going to Chicago."

Everybody looked confused.

"I finally got a ride!" Jack bounced on his toes. His body felt like a rocket ship that was ready to take off.

"That's great news, *niño*," Carlos said.

"It is," Jack agreed. "But now I can't afford to mess up something as easy as *brownies*." He let out a long, wild *arghhh*.

"You just need more practice," Lola said.

She pushed him aside and gathered everyone into a huddle.

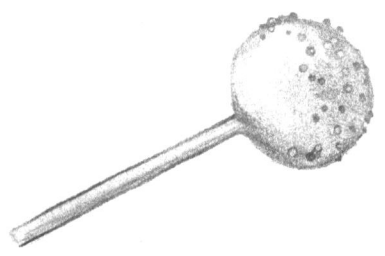

Thirty-Three
Tight Waistbands

After a good deal of whispering, the huddle dispersed, and Lola told Jack they had another challenge for him.

"You need to bake a dozen cake pops," she said. "They should be as bright as a rainbow, but you aren't allowed to use *any* artificial food coloring."

"So how am I supposed to do that?" Jack asked.

"Think outside the box. Channel Ellie, the undisputed queen of substitutions," Theo told him.

Jack nodded. "If she can use bananas in place of eggs, then I can find a replacement for food coloring."

"That's the spirit," Carlos said.

Jack poked around Pogo's kitchen and found a bag of raspberries in the freezer, which he thawed in the microwave and squashed between his fingers. Just as he'd hoped, the juice gave his dough a very pretty tint. It wasn't as vivid as the red in a rainbow, but it was enough to impress his friends.

But then he ran out of time before he could make his frosting.

Lola waggled her braid at him. "You're automatically out on *MMKBC* if you don't finish your challenge."

"I know, I know." Jack thought of all the things he could've done a little faster. He needed to keep a closer eye on the clock.

He'd barely washed the raspberry juice off his hands when his friends huddled again and gave him a third challenge for the night.

"It's the last one, we promise," Lola said.

"It's so fun to torture you, *niño*," Carlos clucked.

"You need to bake a dozen scones," Theo announced. "But not just *any* scones. They need to have a unique flavor profile."

"You guys always use such complicated baking words," Pogo complained.

"It's not complicated at all. A unique flavor profile is just when you use a combination of ingredients that seem random but taste good together," Jack said.

Pogo made a retching noise when Jack mixed dried apricots, sour cream, and orange juice together. "Your scones are gonna be gross, dude."

But Jack was sure his flavor profile would work.

Marvelous Jackson

When the scones were out of the oven and inside everyone's stomachs, Pogo admitted how good they'd turned out. "They're fruity and creamy at the same time. I don't know how you did it."

Jack shrugged. "You saw me do it."

"The glaze on top is really pretty," Lola said.

"I like the little pieces of orange peel," Theo added.

"I like how they crumble into little pieces." Carlos fist-bumped Jack. "You nailed the challenge."

It's about time, Jack thought in relief.

...

Between the brownies, cake pops, and scones that had piled up in their bellies, nobody was hungry for supper.

"I'm gonna bust out of my pants," Carlos moaned.

"My waistband is too tight," Pogo said.

"I'll never eat ever again," Theo wailed.

Jack grinned. He'd done a very good job of feeding his friends.

As everyone packed up to leave Pogo's house, Jack slung his backpack over his shoulder. He said goodbye and headed for the front door, but a small figure blocked his path.

It was Pogo's little sister.

"Hello, Mavis," Jack said.

Mavis scowled. "You and Mikey stole my candy." She

lisped slightly, which Jack attributed to her braces. "The day after Halloween, you broke into my desk and took all my Fudgie Chews and Honey Fizzies."

"You can't eat that stuff anyway because of those brackets on your teeth," Jack said, but he could hear how detestable he sounded. Just because Mavis had braces didn't mean that he and Pogo could go in her room and filch her stuff. It had been his idea, of course. He'd always been the one to push the limit, and he hated the memory of it.

"Seventy-four," Mavis said.

"Seventy-four what?"

"You guys took seventy-four pieces of candy. If you divide it in half, that's thirty-seven pieces each that you and Mikey are responsible for."

"That sounds about right. Sorry. It won't happen again."

"What?" Mavis sputtered.

Jack guessed that she hadn't been expecting an apology of any kind, let alone a sincere one. Not that he could blame her. He'd tormented her for ages and never once said he was sorry. Until now. "I'll pay you back the next time I'm here." He would give her some of the cash he'd gotten from Carlos's mom.

Mavis took a step back. "For real?"

Gently, he patted the top of Mavis's frizzy red head. "For real."

Thirty-Four
Get Outta Town

Jack called Norm as soon as he got home from baking boot camp.

It took six excruciating rings, but Norm finally answered. "Can't talk right now, buddy," he snapped.

"Wait, I just—"

"The dishwasher quit working an hour ago, and we've got ten pounds of knockwurst to boil. It's as hectic as the public boat ramp on the opening morning of walleye season! I need to—"

"*Dad*," Jack said, surprising them both.

Norm fell silent.

"Annabelle can take me to Chicago on Sunday."

"Get outta town," Norm said. "Really?"

"Yep. I can go to my audition."

Norm whooped into the phone. "The barista is saving the day!"

Dusty and Rusty cheered in the background.

"I'll give her free fries for a year!" Norm hollered.

"Holy cow," Jack said. Free fries for a year was nothing to laugh at.

"Do I have to sign a waiver or permission slip or something? You know, so your audition is legal?" Norm asked.

Jack was impressed that Norm had even thought of it. His mom had always handled all the paperwork for their family. "I think it's all taken care of," he replied. Technically, it wasn't a lie.

Norm murmured his assent.

"Hey, I'm going to bike over to Dutch's in a few minutes," Jack said. "I know it's late, but I can wash dishes and boil knockwurst for you."

"But, buddy, it's as cold as a crowbar in the Klondike," Norm said.

"It's fine," Jack replied. He'd never gotten frostbite before, and he wasn't planning to get it anytime soon. "It's the least I can do, seeing as how you guys let me off nuggie duty and found me a ride to *MMKBC*."

Thirty-Five
Dessert Deliveries

Jack's friends were busy the rest of the week, which meant there were no more baking boot camps. He knew he'd have to take matters into his own hands and make every minute count before departing for Chicago.

As if he were cramming for an exam, he pored over his mom's cookbook and memorized as many recipes as he could. He quizzed himself until he knew every ingredient and step.

After giving Mavis a few dollars to pay for the Halloween candy he'd stolen, Jack spent the rest of his Creamy Kalamazoo Cake money at the supermarket to restock his ingredients.

And then, he baked.

He made maple blueberry muffins, buttermilk pound cake, chocolate chess pie, and honey buns.

He gave himself a strict time limit for each project and made sure to check the clock so he could pivot if he started to run out of time.

And when he grew weary from so many challenges, Jack sat on the couch and watched episodes of *MMKBC*.

By now, he'd almost made it through all the seasons, and he couldn't believe there was a chance that he, Jackson Jefferson Wilson, would be chosen as a contestant for the next one.

...

The problem with baking so much was figuring out what to do with everything he made.

Jack filled his backpack with desserts and took them to school. When his friends complained they couldn't take another bite, he gave some to Miss Kibble and even Benny, whose tooth had fully healed.

When Jack handed him a plastic container, Benny looked at it skeptically. "What's this?"

"Rainbow layer cake with vanilla bean frosting."

"Is it—"

"No, it's not poisonous." Jack wondered how many times he'd have to answer that question.

"Uh, thanks?"

"You're welcome." Jack was grateful that Norm had sent Benny's parents a check to pay for the dentist. He and Benny had a clean slate between them now, and he planned to keep it that way.

As Jack left the cafeteria, he accidentally stepped on his loose shoelace, which sent him flying into the arms of Rebecca Danner. He was horrified. Not only was Rebecca the gossip queen of seventh grade, but she was surrounded by her pack of adoring fans.

She squawked and pushed him away.

"Sorry," he mumbled. "Accident."

Before he could slink off in mortification, Rebecca hissed, "Hey, wait! Is it true that you're going to be on a baking show?"

"No," Jack said without missing a beat. *Of course* Rebecca Danner had found out about *MMKBC*. He frowned, thinking about how small Alwyn was, and how fast word got around. He didn't want anyone outside his small circle knowing about his audition, because if he didn't do well or wasn't offered a spot on the next season, then no one could make fun of him.

"That's not what I heard," Rebecca replied.

"Well, you heard wrong."

"That's too bad. For a minute, I thought you were cool." Rebecca looked unimpressed and turned back to her mob of shiny, shallow friends.

"Whatever," Jack said under his breath. He hadn't taken up baking as a hobby to impress anybody else—especially not Rebecca Danner.

...

After school, Jack biked to Dutch's.

Dusty and Rusty were happy to accept all the desserts he'd brought, and in return they presented him with a royal blue t-shirt that said *DUTCH'S A-1 TAVERN: PERFECTING POULTRY SINCE 1996*. Under the words was a smiling nuggie wearing a superhero cape.

"Dusty ordered these for us," Rusty said. "We're gonna wear them Sunday so we look like a real team. Even though you won't be there, Jackal, you'll be with us in spirit. You did a lot to help us prepare."

Jack felt a lump form in his throat, and he tried to clear his voice. "I wish I could be in two places at once," he squeaked as he took the t-shirt.

"We do, too," Dusty said. "But you're going after your dream."

"Thanks for having my back." Jack knew that without Dusty and Rusty, he wouldn't be going anywhere.

...

On Friday after school, Jack ran his last dessert delivery of the week.

He rode to the library and parked his bike in the rack, just like a regular person. He didn't want to stow it in the woods anymore. What was the point? His mom didn't work there, and he wasn't planning to have any more sleepovers under the card catalog.

He walked up to the plaque in the lobby and spoke quietly. "Hi, Mom. I just wanted to say thanks for sharing your cookbook, apron, and platters with me. You're the best."

He gave the plaque a quick rub and headed to the circulation desk, where Miss Holzhacker was organizing books. Jack hadn't seen her since the night she'd made those awful comments about him.

"Hello," he said, crisply.

She gave a haughty shrug. "Hello."

"Is Miss Jean Ann here?"

"She's catching up on paperwork. May I tell her who's asking?"

"Jack." *Even though you knew that already.*

Miss Holzhacker disappeared into the back office, and Miss Jean Ann came running out a second later. "Is it true?" she asked him, wild-eyed.

"Is what true?"

"Yesterday I was at Hardworking Hank's Hardware Shop, and I overheard somebody saying you might be on that famous baking show in Chicago."

Jack leaned over the counter. "It's true," he whispered.

Miss Jean Ann slapped her palms to her cheeks. "That's *amazing*."

"I know, but I'm trying to keep it on the down low since I might not get chosen to be on the next season."

"My lips are sealed." Miss Jean Ann made a zipping motion in front of her mouth. "What're your odds of making it?"

"Thirty-six of us are auditioning on Sunday, and twelve will get picked."

"Gosh, I'm so proud of you."

"Well, you got me started by showing me the best cookbooks for beginners."

"I was just doing my job, but it was a pleasure." Miss Jean Ann's cheeks were flushed. "Is your dad taking you to Chicago?"

Jack shook his head. "The Northwoods nuggie competition is the same day, so we have to split up."

"Oh, right." A sad expression flashed across her face. "Who's driving you, then?"

"Annabelle, who owns Hug in a Mug. Her brother Dusty works at Dutch's. She has to pick up coffee beans in Bucktown, so she offered to take me."

"Annabelle makes great lattes, but is she keeping a close eye on the weather forecast?"

"What do you mean?"

"It's supposed to snow all weekend."

"It always snows around here. No big deal."

"But this will be the first snowfall of the season that sticks."

Marvelous Jackson

Jack shrugged.

"I'm hosting my sister's baby shower on Sunday, and I'm beginning to worry that no one will be able to make it."

"I'm sure it'll be OK," Jack said. Maybe he and Annabelle would have to hit the road earlier than planned, but he didn't mind. Missing out on sleep wasn't a problem.

He reached into his backpack and pulled out a few baggies. "I brought you some treats."

Miss Holzhacker came up behind Miss Jean Ann.

"Would you like some, too?" he asked, inwardly cringing. He didn't love the idea of being nice to her, but he knew he could be the bigger person.

"Heavens, no. I don't eat sugar." Miss Holzhacker wrinkled her nose.

Of course you don't. Jack desperately wanted to roll his eyes, but he'd avoided the habit for so long now, it didn't seem worth the energy.

Miss Holzhacker went back to her books, and Miss Jean Ann skirted the circulation desk so that she and Jack were face-to-face. She embraced him fiercely and whispered in his ear, "You are marvelous, Jackson."

Jack returned her hug.

Outside, as he unlocked his bike, he brushed a tickle off his nose, and another off his forehead.

He looked up at the swirling, pink-tinged dome above him.

Snowflakes.

It was just a dusting. It would be fine.

Thirty-Six
No Big Deal

Later that night, Jack was in the middle of baking Pfeffernüsse cookies for his carnic with Annabelle when his phone buzzed. He fished it out of his pocket with fingers that smelled like cardamom.

The text was from her. *Jack, we have a BIG problem.*

"She'd better not be freaking out over the weather," he muttered, even though the snow had only gotten worse.

Jack

> What's up?

Annabelle

> I've come down with the flu!

"The flu?" Jack yelled. He hadn't been expecting that. "How bad can the flu be?"

> **Annabelle**
> My stomach hurts like crazy. I can't keep any food or water down. Every time I stand up, I feel dizzy and weak.

Jack didn't know what to say. He wanted—he *needed*—Annabelle to feel better, right away. She was his ride!

> **Annabelle**
> At the rate I'm going, there's no way I can leave my bed this weekend, let alone drive to Chicago.

"Oh, no," Jack whimpered. He began pacing the kitchen.

> **Annabelle**
> I'm so, so sorry for stranding you. I feel awful about it.

"This cannot be happening," Jack said. He wanted to gnash his teeth or rip out his hair.

Marvelous Jackson

Annabelle

I even asked my parents if they could take you, but they're concerned about the weather. They're very sad they can't help.

"I need a ride!" Jack wailed. He forced himself to breathe deeply, and he replied to Annabelle with all the fake cheer he could muster.

Jack

I'm sorry about you getting the flu, I hope you feel better soon, please don't worry about my ride, I'll figure something out

He knew it wasn't Annabelle's fault that she was sick, but he wanted to scream. He couldn't believe how far he'd come, only to have his transportation fall apart at the last minute!

The inside of his brain felt buzzy and hot, just like when he'd tripped Benny and smacked Theo's locker. It should have served as a warning, but Jack ignored it. Instead, he swept his arm across the kitchen table, sending flour, German spices, and mixing bowls shooting in all directions. Everything banged and clattered against the cabinets and floor.

"I wasted everybody's time and money!" he yelled, thinking of the awesome boot camps his friends had put together and all the ingredients they'd bought for him.

He marched over to the wall that he'd damaged, back when he'd burned his Sugar Dumplings. He knew that underneath the Cover-It-Up, there would always be a chip of paint that was missing.

He screwed his hand into a tight coil and pulled his arm back, as if he were getting ready to throw a football. His fist shot forward, and he anticipated the searing pain that was to come.

Only, he couldn't follow through.

An inch from the wall, his hand froze, trembling like the very last leaf on the tree outside.

Thirty-Seven
A Frigid Friday Night in the Far North of Wisconsin

Jack crumpled to the floor. He hugged his hand to his chest, even though he hadn't injured it. In a fit of anger, he'd risked so much—and nearly lost it all.

He'd come dangerously close, but he was so glad that he hadn't punched a hole in the wall.

A tear leaked from his eye and trickled down his cheek. He groped around for his phone. Amidst the chaos, it had landed a few feet away. He needed Clare.

Jack

> My ride to Chicago just fell through! I can't audition!

He didn't expect her to text back because it was so late, but his phone buzzed instantly.

> **Clare**
> What do you mean you don't have a ride? There must be someone else you can ask! You can't miss your audition!

Jack explained how Annabelle had been planning to take him, but she'd gotten sick.

> **Clare**
> What about Theo and Lola? Or Carlos or Pogo? Couldn't one of their parents drive you?

> **Jack**
> I don't know, this all just happened, and I haven't had a chance to ask them yet. Isn't it too late to text them right now?

> **Clare**
> You texted me . . .

> **Jack**
> Good point

Marvelous Jackson

Clare
Even if they don't get your message until tomorrow, you've got nothing to lose. You can't throw away your shot.

Jack
OK, fine . . .

Clare
You'll thank me later.

Jack hoped she was right. He clicked on their group text, which by now was filled with tons of messages—not just about baking, but about everyone else's hobbies as well. Like deer hunting, Drama Club, swim team, and fungi. They'd shared so many jokes, stories, and information, it felt like they'd all known each other forever.

Jack ran his fingers through his snarled hair and sent out his plea for help.

...

Next, Jack messaged Norm, Dusty, and Rusty.

He had no idea if they knew Annabelle was sick, but he needed to share the news. Maybe there was a tiny chance that one of them would offer to bow out of the nuggie competition and drive him to Chicago.

When he got no response, he began to clean up the Pfeffernüsse mess. The kitchen was a disaster, but he knew it would've been even worse if he'd punched the wall.

No road trip with Annabelle. No audition. No chance to be on MMKBC. *No twenty-thousand-dollar prize.*

He wanted to shake himself awake and find that it was all a terrible dream, but he knew it was wishful thinking.

It was almost midnight by the time he climbed into bed. He felt as pathetic and limp as the miserable lettuce at Lunkers. As he pulled his navy blanket over his head, he checked his phone and frowned. He *still* hadn't heard back from Norm, Dusty, or Rusty. They always kept their phones turned on. And why wasn't Norm home yet?

Jack dialed his dad's number, but it rang and rang before going to voicemail.

He called Dusty. And then Rusty. Same thing: voicemail.

Jack couldn't imagine where they were or what they were doing. Why would all of them be ignoring his calls and messages?

He put his hand on his stomach. He wanted to push the rising unease back down, but it was already spreading through his body. He pressed a little harder, and that's when he heard a far-off siren. Clanging, insistent, unmistakable.

Jack kicked off his blanket and bolted out of bed. He ran to the front door of the cottage and threw it open.

Marvelous Jackson

It wasn't just one siren. It was two, maybe three, and it sounded like they were all heading downtown.

He was sure of it: something was wrong.

He needed to find Norm.

Jack pulled on a hoodie and hurried outside. Thank goodness for his handlebar light! He climbed on his bike and rode into the frigid Friday night in the far north of Wisconsin.

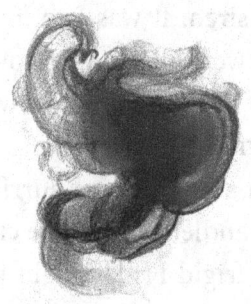

Thirty-Eight
A Crying Shame

As he followed the sound of sirens, Jack realized he'd never been out so late before, on his bicycle, by himself. He pedaled up and down rolling hills, through the woods, and around Lake Alwyn and Lake Lyons. He passed by Evergreen School and shivered at the sight of the looming, unlit building and silvery white football field.

His teeth chattered, and he clutched his wet, chilly handlebars tighter. He was positive that if he got off his bike and leaned over the side of the road, he'd throw up a small mound of **Pfeffernüsse dough**.

As he approached downtown Alwyn, car headlights began to punctuate the darkness. He couldn't understand why people were out, but the closer Jack got to Main Street, the more everything made sense.

Marvelous Jackson

He smelled smoke.

It was becoming harder and harder to pedal through the falling snow. His legs felt like thick, wooden clubs, but Jack knew he couldn't stop.

At the end of the street, he saw furious black puffs rising into the sky, directly above Dutch's, and the shouts of firefighters and police officers filled the air.

Oh, no. Oh, no. Oh, no. What if Dad is hurt?

But as soon as Jack pulled into the parking lot, he saw Norm flailing and yelling. Weak with relief, he almost rode his bike straight into his dad.

"Buddy, why on earth are you here?" Norm shouted. "You should be at home, safe in bed!"

Jack tried to absorb the scene before him: Dutch's had been reduced to a smoldering version of its former self. He couldn't see anything from the restaurant he'd known his entire life. Not the wood-paneled walls, or the mounted deer heads, or the old kitchen with Dusty and Rusty cooking in their white chef coats—

"Are Dusty and Rusty OK?" he yelled.

Norm nodded. "Everyone's fine." He gestured at the pack of people that had amassed, and sure enough, Dusty and Rusty were among them, looking sodden and grim.

It seemed to Jack as if half the town had rolled out of bed to get a front-row seat for the fire. Most of them wore pajamas under their parkas, and they blew on their mittened hands and stomped their boot-clad feet to stay warm.

Jack climbed off his bike and wiped away the ice crystals that had formed on his eyelashes. "What happened?"

Norm swiped a hand over his stunned, ashy face. "We'd just locked up for the night and were heading home. I was almost at the cottage when my phone rang. It was Officer Frankenmuth, saying that Dutch's had gone up in flames, so I turned around and came right back. Dusty and Rusty did, too."

"But how did a fire start *after* you guys left? It's not as if anybody was here, cooking."

"That's what we're trying to figure out." Norm looked haggard.

Jack pointed. "Speaking of Officer Frankenmuth."

The portly policeman approached them, carrying a notepad in one hand and a walkie-talkie in the other. "It's a crying shame what's happened to Dutch's, Norman, but I'm glad to report that Detective Steiner has successfully apprehended the perpetrators."

"The perpetrators?" Norm echoed.

"You betcha. Couple guys from Illinois. Filthy rich. They came up north to enjoy our winter wonderland, but they got carried away. Right after you fellas locked up for the night, they drove into the parking lot in their Jeep and started doin' donuts in the snow."

"Donuts?" Jack and Norm said in unison.

"They were making tight, slippery turns, spinning

round and round. But they lost control of the Jeep and ran smack into a utility pole." Officer Frankenmuth pointed toward the spot where the utility pole once stood. "It fell over and landed on the roof, and Dutch's went up in flames, just like kindling."

"Holy cow," Jack breathed.

"The guys fled the scene of the crime, but they did the right thing and just turned themselves in," Officer Frankenmuth said. "Funny thing is, they love your restaurant. They told Detective Steiner that they eat at Dutch's every time they're in Alwyn. Said you got the best onion rings north of the pressure line."

Norm lifted his chin. "Well, they're right about that."

Jack slung his arm around his dad's quaking shoulders.

"Come on down to the station, Norman, and we'll get everything sorted out," Officer Frankenmuth said. "We'll have to file some reports and do a bunch of paperwork, but at least it'll be dry and toasty in my office. I'll see you soon, OK?"

Norm nodded, and the policeman walked back to his squad car.

A minute later, a hand alighted on Jack's back. He would know its butterfly-like sensation anywhere.

"Hello, Jackson. Hello, Norman." Miss Jean Ann's cheeks were ruddy, and under her puffy jacket she wore red-and-white striped pajama pants that reminded Jack of candy canes. "I'm so sorry about the fire."

"Excuse me, excuse me!" A small figure pushed into their little knot and pointed a gloved finger at Jack that reminded him of a talon. "You!"

"Me?" Jack said. What was Miss Holzhacker doing there?

"What's this hullaballoo all about?" she shrieked. "The noise! The smoke! And it's past my bedtime! Couldn't you keep it down?"

"Um," Jack replied. "None of this is my fault?"

"I couldn't help but notice your bike tracks winding across town on my way here. I followed them right to this very parking lot. You're out past curfew, young man, and it's not safe to be riding a bicycle in all this precipitation." Miss Holzhacker pinched up her entire face. "You're not even wearing a winter coat! What is *wrong* with you?"

"Hey, now, wait a minute," Norm said. "That's my kid, and there's nothing wrong with—"

"*You!*" Now she pointed her finger at Norm.

"Me?" Norm looked startled.

"I remember you from fifth grade. You were in my class at Cranberry Marsh Elementary. No other student in the school had as many suspensions as you did! No wonder your son reminded me of someone. He reminded me of *you*."

Norm made a perfect O with his mouth as he realized who he was talking to. "Why, it's nice to see you again, Miss Holzhacker. It's been a long time, hasn't it?"

Marvelous Jackson

Jack couldn't believe it. Norm had been Miss Holzhacker's student! *My poor dad*, he thought.

Miss Holzhacker rolled her eyes at them. "Like father, like son."

Miss Jean Ann held up her hands. "As you can see, Miss Holzhacker, Alwyn's finest restaurant has just burned down, which means there are *far* more important matters for us to deal with. No one has the energy to worry about curfews, winter coats, or grade-school suspensions from thirty years ago. Why don't you head on home and warm up?"

Miss Holzhacker stormed off, and Norm called out, "Thank you for helping to mold young lives in our community!"

Jack heard the bite of sarcasm in Norm's words, and if Dutch's didn't have smoke above it, he would've given his dad a high five.

"Everything's a mess," Norm wailed, once Miss Holzhacker was out of sight. "I've lost my wife, my restaurant, and the nuggie competition."

"Why the nuggie competition?" Jack asked him.

"I don't have my recipe card or my ingredients. It's all destroyed!"

"You're wrong," Jack said, not unkindly. "You don't need your recipe card because I've got the whole thing memorized, and we can buy all your ingredients at the supermarket."

Norm stood stock-still. "You know my recipe by heart?"

Jack nodded. He'd helped develop it, after all. It would be imprinted in his brain forever.

Norm looked joyful, but then his face fell. "How can I be happy about that right now with your ride to Chicago falling through? I got your texts about Annabelle, and I'm so sorry."

"Oh, no," Miss Jean Ann murmured. "What happened?"

"She's got the flu and can't take me to my audition," Jack explained.

"I would drive you if I didn't have to host my sister's baby shower!"

Knowing that she would've helped if she could was almost as good as getting an actual ride from her.

"What do you say we get out of here, buddy? I can't handle any more of this madness," Norm said.

Jack, too, was sick of the noise, smoke, and snow.

"We can throw your bike in the back of my truck. I'll drop you off at home on my way to the police station."

"OK. I'll—" Jack started to say, but there was a crash, and together they watched what was left of Dutch's cave in on itself.

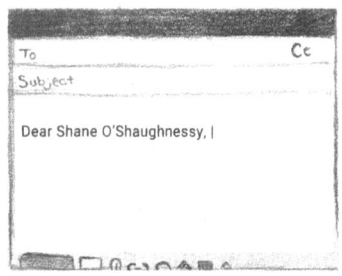

Thirty-Nine
Gonna Be a Long Day

"What a night," Norm sighed as he pulled up to the cottage.

"I can't believe it's four a.m." Jack's eyes watered as he yawned.

"I hope you can get some rest."

"I will, but I'm sorry you have to go to the police station."

"While I'm there, I'll think real hard of anybody who might be able to drive you to Chicago. I'll start making phone calls once the sun is up."

Jack was surprised that Norm had any energy left to think about *MMKBC*. As Dutch's had burned, Jack had bid farewell to any remaining hope of making it to the studio. "I can't audition—not with us losing the restaurant like that. It's not a great time for me to be going anywhere."

Norm reached over and ruffled Jack's hair. "If we can find you a ride, you gotta go."

Jack buried his face in his hands. For so long, he'd felt like Norm had cared only about Dutch's, but now that the restaurant was gone, Jack could see how much *he* had loved it, too. He regretted all the times he'd complained about Norm's busy schedule, the steamy kitchen, and the endless carryout boxes. He couldn't imagine his dad working anywhere else.

Norm attempted to brush the ashes off his brown canvas jacket, but he only made the grimy smears worse. "Not all hope is lost. I'm sure we'll get insurance money. If we can, we'll rebuild. We'll figure something out."

"I hope so," Jack said.

"Now get inside where it's warm. I'll let you know if I get any leads on transportation."

"OK," Jack said, but he was already thinking about the email he would send to Shane O'Shaughnessy, explaining how he wouldn't be able to make it to the studio the next morning. It would be a horrible message to write, but not nearly as horrible as losing Dutch's. "Good luck at the police station."

"I'm afraid it's gonna be a long day for your old man."

Jack put his hand on Norm's shoulder and said, "You've got this." He got out of the truck and waved goodbye as his dad drove away.

Marvelous Jackson

In the gray, smudgy light of a distant daybreak, he let himself into the cottage, peeled off his smelly clothes, and fell into bed like a fifty-pound bag of flour.

Forty
For Real This Time

When Jack woke a few hours later, the sun was up, but it was blocked by clouds that resembled slabs of concrete. The snow had stopped, but he guessed it was only a matter of time before it started up again.

Not that it mattered.

I'm not going to Chicago, so we can have a blizzard for all I care.

He decided to spend the day helping Norm, Dusty, and Rusty with nuggie stuff. He would offer to go to the supermarket to buy ingredients, and he'd write out copies of the recipe for everybody.

Maybe he could hang out with his friends, too, and bake them something special as a way of saying thanks for everything they'd done to support him.

Marvelous Jackson

But first, a shower.

He shuffled into the bathroom and used every drop of scalding water in the cottage to scrub the stink and grime off his skin. When he climbed out of the shower a little while later, his phone was buzzing like mad. Dripping wet, he swiped at the screen and saw that his friends were in a texting frenzy.

"What the . . . ?"

He began scrolling through the messages.

The first texts were about the fire, of course, because everyone had heard about it. Alwyn was small, and word got around fast, even at the crack of dawn on a Saturday.

But then his friends changed gears.

Clare

Now—for some good news, Prez . . .

Theo

We can take you to your audition today! Me and Lola and our moms! I repeat: WE CAN DRIVE YOU TO CHICAGO!

"What?" Clumsily, Jack sat on the edge of the bathtub, his knees vibrating.

> **Lola**
> Abby has to teach a boxing class, so we can't leave until she's done at 5

> **Theo**
> More snow is on the way, but our moms say we'll have plenty of time to make it to Clare's house

"Clare's house?" Jack couldn't believe he'd get to see where she lived.

More to the point, he couldn't believe he'd get to see *her*.

> **Clare**
> Everyone will spend the night

> **Lola**
> And in the morning, we'll take you to the MMKBC studio

> **Clare**
> It's downtown, not too far from Morrissey

Marvelous Jackson

Carlos

There's not enough room in the Porters' car for me and Pogo, so we're stuck here in Alwyn, but we're gonna volunteer to help your dad at the nuggie competition—not that I know anything about nuggies

Pogo

Me neither, but we can learn, because Jack has showed us that anybody can do anything

Jack tried to smooth his wet hair, which smelled strongly of shampoo, but his hands weren't working the way they were supposed to. Was it bad that he was leaving Norm so soon after the fire? Could he turn down his friends, who had **concocted an entire plan on his behalf?**

I'll do whatever Norm tells me to do, he decided.

Jack

I can't believe it, I got a ride to Chicago

Norm

No way! With who?

> **Jack**
> My friends Lola and Theo Porter and their moms

Jack told Norm they were planning to leave at five o'clock, spend the night at Clare's house in Morrissey, and return to Alwyn after his audition.

> **Norm**
> Sounds like a great plan. I'm so glad you're going, buddy.

> **Jack**
> You sure?

> **Norm**
> Sure as the lakes freezing by Christmas!

> **Jack**
> Are you OK at the police station?

> **Norm**
> So far so good. Dusty and Rusty are here, too. We're figuring out details for the nuggie competition, and we've decided we're all committed to rebuilding Dutch's. We're going to make it work, no matter what.

Marvelous Jackson

Jack almost slid off the side of the bathtub in relief. His dad was in good spirits. Norm, Dusty, and Rusty would fry up the best chicken in the Northwoods, and Dutch's would make a comeback, even if it looked a little different than before.

Still wrapped in his towel, Jack scrambled to type out the nuggie recipe for Norm. He reviewed it to make sure there were no mistakes, and then he hit *SEND*.

"I'm going to *MMKBC*," he breathed. "I'm going to *MMKBC* for real this time."

He texted his friends. *This is an awesome plan. Thank you. You're all the best.* And for the next hour, their messages flew back and forth like a flock of agitated birds. He'd never seen any of them so excited before.

When their texting flurry was done, Jack packed for his trip to Chicago. He tossed pajamas, underwear, deodorant, a toothbrush, and a hoodie in his backpack. Then he added hair gel, a comb, and the button-down shirt he'd worn for his *MMKBC* application video.

Now what? he wondered.

Staying busy was the only thing that would keep him from thinking about his stomach, which felt like it was performing a gymnastics routine, so he shoveled the driveway and the front steps of the cottage, which were still covered in snow. He even threw out the pot of dead geraniums that had turned to dust so long ago. Then he went back inside and baked a batch of shortbread cookies to share with the Porters.

Finally, it was 4:55 p.m.

Five minutes was all that was left until the journey of his lifetime would begin.

Jack sent Norm one last message. *Getting ready to head out. Good luck at the nuggie competition. You'll be great.*

There was a honk in the driveway.

He threw his backpack over his shoulder and ran out into the cold.

Forty-One
Precious Cargo

Abby had been driving for barely an hour when snow began to tumble from the sky. The flakes were as fat as cotton balls and kept clumping together on the windshield. She turned on the wipers to their fastest setting, but it didn't make a difference. "I knew the weather was going to be bad, but this is *rough*," she said, giving her cropped blonde hair a shake.

"We've got plenty of time. The Burches will wait up for us, no matter how late it is," Marisa told her.

Jack, Theo, and Lola were smooshed together in the back seat. They tried to see out the windows, but it was official: they were in the middle of a whiteout.

Abby slowed the car to a crawl.

"Should we . . . should we go back to Alwyn?" Jack could hardly get the words out. There was nothing he wanted *less* than to turn around, but he felt guilty that the Porters were driving through a blizzard on his account.

"Absolutely not," Marisa said. "We'll get you there safely, I promise."

Abby continued their trek southward. "Slow and steady wins the prize."

Mile by mile, the drive to Chicago grew more treacherous. They'd move a few feet and then stop until their headlights cut a path through the plummeting snow.

"Remind me again why we didn't we take my pickup truck?" Abby said.

"Not good for city driving," Marisa replied.

Jack saw Abby licking her lips nervously in the light of the dashboard, but she refused to pull over. "We're ferrying precious cargo. It's *MMKBC* or bust."

Me? Precious cargo? Jack smiled in the dark.

...

"How's your dad doing?" Marisa asked Jack a little while later. "It's so awful, what happened to his restaurant."

"He's been at the police station all day, so I haven't seen him, but he texted me earlier to say that he's planning to rebuild Dutch's, which is great news." Jack checked his phone, but there weren't any other messages or calls from Norm. "He's getting geared up for the nuggie competition tomorrow, so I'm sure he's super busy."

Marvelous Jackson

Over the next hour, the inside of the car grew quieter and quieter, minus the crunch of **shortbread cookies**, the rhythmic thwap of the windshield wipers, and the sputter of snow on the highway.

Marisa called Clare's mom to tell her they were running late—*really* late. According to the clock on the dashboard, it was nearly midnight, and they hadn't even made it out of Wisconsin.

Jack couldn't believe how long they'd been driving. As Saturday night tipped toward Sunday morning, all he wanted to do was close his eyes.

"I need some music to pump me up," Abby murmured to Marisa.

Next thing Jack knew, the comforting caterwaul of Bacillus Maximus throbbed quietly from the speakers.

Abby tapped the steering wheel in time with the drumbeat. "I love these guys."

Marisa giggled. "They're certainly an acquired taste."

I love them, too, Abby! Jack wanted to say, but he was too tired to speak.

As the song came to an end, he couldn't help it: his head lolled over onto Theo's shoulder. Theo's head slumped on top of Jack's, and Lola began to snore.

Before surrendering to sleep, Jack pictured the stylish, modern *MMKBC* kitchen. Although the distance between him and the studio was slowly shrinking, it still felt so far away.

Forty-Two
Skyline

Lola nudged Jack with her knee. "Wake up, Jackers."

Jack rolled out his neck and rubbed his eyes.

"We're here! We're in Chicago!" she whispered.

He squinted through the car window into a morning that was crystal clear and dazzling. It was like being inside a snow globe; after too much shaking, the swirling flakes had finally settled.

Marisa was behind the wheel now, and Abby was asleep in the passenger seat.

"We switched places a couple hours ago," Marisa said, glancing at Jack in the rearview mirror. "It took us more than twice as long to get here, but we made it."

"We have to go straight downtown to the studio," Lola told Jack.

"No sleepover at Clare's house?" Theo whined, rousing himself awake.

Marvelous Jackson

"It's already morning, Theodore. We'll see Clare after we drop off Jack," Marisa said.

But not me. I won't be able to see her now. Jack felt a little ache in his chest, but the more pressing concern was that he probably looked like a wreck from his long night in the back seat.

"Look!" Marisa pointed.

Far ahead, at the end of the glittering freeway, was the city skyline. Angular buildings were stacked tightly, side by side, and Jack knew that beyond the offices, apartments, and restaurants was mighty Lake Michigan. Deep and icy, it would make Lake Alwyn and Lake Lyons look like mere droplets of water.

"Chicago," he breathed. He couldn't believe how far he'd come.

"I'm sorry you won't have a chance to wash up, but I grabbed you a breakfast sandwich and something to drink at the last gas station." Marisa passed a paper bag back to Jack.

Strangely, he wasn't hungry at all, but he forced himself to gnaw on the egg sandwich and wash it down with the container of milk. The sandwich was cold, and the milk was warm, but he needed calories to fuel him through everything that lay ahead.

He attempted to comb his hair, which was pointing in all directions like vicious little daggers, and then he pulled the button-down shirt out of his backpack.

"Jack!" Theo shrieked, waking Abby. "That looks like it's for a first grader." He burst into laughter.

Jack balled up the shirt and threw it at Theo.

Theo giggled and threw it back. "It's even too small for me!"

"Just wear your hoodie," Lola said to Jack. "Be you."

Jack nodded.

He had no other option, and for once, that was OK by him.

Forty-Three
Until I Caught Up with You

Marisa pulled up in front of a squat brown building. "Is this it?"

Abby's head bobbed enthusiastically as she checked the map on her phone. "I'm thrilled to report we've officially made it to the headquarters for *The Marvelous Midwest Kids Baking Championship*!"

The entire car burst into applause. Lola whistled, Theo waved his hands in the air, and Abby and Marisa gave each other high fives.

"Thank you so much for driving me," Jack said, once the commotion died down. "I never would've gotten to Chicago without you all."

"Do you think they'll let us park here for a few minutes so we can go in with Jack? I refuse to just drop him off and drive away," Marisa said to Abby.

Abby climbed out of the passenger seat and approached the security guard patrolling the front of the building. She said something to him and gestured toward the car. Finally, the security guard gave a curt nod. Jack figured he'd noticed how strong and imposing Abby was and didn't want to argue with someone who could squash him like an insect.

Abby returned to the car. "The security guard said we can leave it here for a few minutes. Let's go."

They spilled out into the gleaming white winter day. The millions of fallen snowflakes were like tiny mirrors, reflecting the sun back to Jack. He wondered if the *MMKBC* studio lights would be just as bright.

The security guard held the spotless glass door open for them, and they went inside.

Jack couldn't believe how big and bright the lobby was. Colorful *MMKBC* signs and banners hung from the walls, along with huge photographs of past and current contestants.

"Look, it's Ruby!" Marisa said.

"And Otis!" Theo said.

"And Ellie!" Jack said.

"You're all obsessed," Lola scoffed, but she pointed at one of the photographs, too. "It's Roscoe!"

The glass door of the lobby opened again, and to Jack's astonishment, Clare ran in, along with her mom and grandmother. Their cheeks were rosy, and thick scarves whipped behind them.

Marvelous Jackson

The Burches and the Porters greeted each other with hugs and loud squeals that ricocheted off the high ceilings and glossy floors. Jack suddenly felt too tall, and he didn't know what to do with his hands. He wondered why he hadn't thought to get a haircut.

"Prez!" Clare cried, making him jump. "I'm so glad we made it in time to wish you good luck." She tried to throw her arms around him, but it was impossible, because tiny Roger was buried in the folds of her puffy coat. "We need to keep him hidden, because pets aren't allowed," she whispered. "But he wanted to say hi."

Jack hadn't seen Roger since his horrible mistake with the BB gun over the summer, when he'd been terrified that he'd accidentally killed him. Now, Jack leaned forward to bury his face in Roger's soft brown hair. "Hi there, little guy. I'm so sorry I hurt you. It'll never happen again."

Roger licked the tear that leaked from Jack's eye.

A woman wearing a business suit and headset walked into the lobby, her pointy high heels going clickety-clack, and Clare tucked Roger away.

"Welcome, welcome. I'm Betsy, the producer for *The Marvelous Midwest Kids Baking Championship*. Is one of you Jackson?"

Everyone quieted as Jack gave an awkward wave.

"You're the last baker to arrive," she said. "We've got an impressive group assembled for our auditions, including kids from Cleveland, Lansing, South Bend, Springfield, and Ames, but you're the only one who had to drive through that nasty Wisconsin blizzard. It's a miracle you got here in one piece."

You have no idea, Jack thought.

Betsy pulled a square of soft, light-gray fabric from the clipboard she was carrying and handed it to Jack. "You're going to need this."

He shook it open. It was an apron, with *The Marvelous Midwest Kids Baking Championship* embroidered across the front, along with his entire name: *Jackson Jefferson Wilson*.

Jack had worn a blaze orange apron at Dutch's, Marisa's red apron at Theo's house, and his mom's lacy apron at home, but he'd never had his own before. He tied the gray *MMKBC* apron around his neck and felt an inch taller.

"Looks great on you. Shane will be thrilled to see you wearing it," Betsy said.

"Did you say Shane? As in Shane O'Shaughnessy?" Marisa looked at Betsy with a starstruck expression.

"You bet. Mister Popularity is back in the studio right now."

Marisa gave a dreamy sigh.

Betsy gestured at the Porters and Burches. "I'm assuming this is your family, Jack?"

"Something like that," he replied, and he felt them shift a little closer, as if forming a protective, tender circle around him.

Betsy paged through the papers on her clipboard. "Is one of you Norman Wilson? He's the adult listed on your permission slip."

Jack shifted from one foot to the other. "Well, no. Not exactly."

At that moment, the glass door of the lobby flew open. A gust of wintry air shot in from the street—along with Norm himself.

"*Dad?*" Jack said.

Norm's face was unshaven, and he was wearing the same sooty clothes as the day before. "I made it!" he yelled, sliding through the gigantic puddle that everyone's wet shoes had made. He flew into Jack's arms. "I made it! Thank you, Porters, for driving my son!"

Jack shook his head in disbelief. "You're supposed to be at the nuggie competition!"

"*Nuggie competition?*" Betsy murmured.

"Are you kidding?" Norm said. "Being with you is more important than frying lumps of chicken. Dusty and Rusty have your recipe, and everything's under control. If anyone can win, it's them."

Jack's eyes widened. "You left Dusty and Rusty in charge?"

"I also asked them to be co-owners of Dutch's with me! Shoulda done it sooner. We'll oversee the new construction together, and once it's done, we'll divide up all the shifts and hire more employees to help us. I can't run the restaurant on my own anymore. I need more time with you, so we can figure out how to be a family of two."

Jack felt a little breathless. His dad was finally ready to make a big change in his life.

"Everybody's at the Piney Point Expo Center right now, including your buddies Pogo and Carlos. I was hoping to get some updates from them, but would you believe I lost my phone?" Norm gave a sheepish grin.

"Is that why you haven't called or texted?" Jack asked.

Norm nodded. "I dropped it somewhere in the snow in Alwyn, probably when I was leaving the police station. I wanted to call the Porters and tell them to turn around so I could drive you instead, but I had no way of reaching them."

Jack pulled his arms around himself and squeezed.

"There wasn't one minute to lose," Norm continued. "Right away, I started heading south. I went straight through that blizzard, and I promised myself I wouldn't stop until I caught up with you."

"I'm so glad you made it," Jack said.

"But how were you able to find our studio without a map?" Betsy asked. Her eyebrows were two dark triangles.

"I stopped along the way and asked for help." Norm shrugged. "There are some real nice Illinois folks out there."

"Of course there are," Betsy said, looking miffed.

"One last thing, buddy," Norm went on. "Annabelle called me earlier, before I lost my phone. She asked if it would be all right to hire you for a couple hours each week. Hug in a Mug needs sweet treats, and she's no good at baking. Dusty's been sharing your desserts with her, and she's a fan."

"But I told you that I would work at Dutch's once my audition is over."

"I know, but Dutch's doesn't have cookies or scones on the menu. A coffee shop is where you belong."

Jack grinned and scraped his hand through his hair—until he remembered he was trying to keep it neat for his audition. Hurriedly, he pushed it back in place.

Betsy cleared her voice to get everyone's attention. "I know Shane's eager to get started with the auditions, but there's something I need to show you all first."

The lobby lights dimmed.

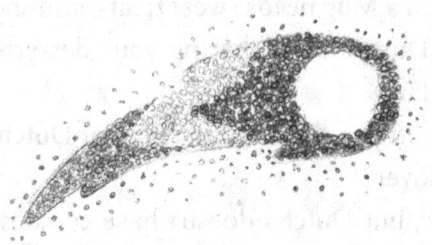

Forty-Four
Knock Their Socks Off, Jackson

A large, white screen descended from the ceiling, and the *MMKBC* theme song began to play.

Um, hi. My name is Jackson Jefferson Wilson, but you can call me Jack.

"Holy cow, that's from my audition video!" Jack exclaimed.

Sure enough, there he was, sitting at his kitchen table, wearing his shrunken button-down shirt. His face looked so enormous, he could see the smattering of pores across his nose.

"How embarrassing," he started to say, but he stopped. It wasn't embarrassing at all. He'd accomplished something that only thirty-five other kids in the Midwest had pulled off.

Marvelous Jackson

"Did you make one of these videos for every baker who's here today?" Norm asked Betsy.

She nodded. "We watched them earlier, when everyone else was arriving."

"Will you include them in the first episode of the next season? To introduce viewers to the new contestants?" Marisa's eyes shone like two little lanterns.

"You know the drill," Betsy replied.

Oh, I hope that's me, Jack thought, bouncing on his toes. *I want to be one of the new contestants more than anything.*

But he knew that if he wasn't chosen—if he never, ever competed on a big-hearted, **world-famous, award-winning** baking show—he had achieved something remarkable. He was proud of himself, and maybe that was what mattered most in the end.

The video continued.

> *I live in a small town in northern Wisconsin. Almost everybody here hunts and goes fishing, but I'm not into that kind of stuff. I don't love being outside, and I've got bad aim, so don't give me a slingshot or BB gun unless you want me to shoot off one of your toes.*
>
> *I've never really fit in, and things only got worse after my mom died, four hundred and . . . well, I can't remember how many days it's been anymore, which is good, because keeping track used to be the only*

thing I was decent at. And playing Candy Smash. *I did something really bad at school to a guy named Benny, and I found out from the principal that I had to change my ways, or I'd end up getting kicked out of Evergreen for good. It was the worst feeling, but then things started to change.*

It began with me making a new friend. Theo invited me over to his house, and we made cookies. It sounds basic, but I hadn't done anything like that in a long time, and it brought back great memories of baking with my mom.

Thanks to Theo and his family, I realized how fun, and challenging, and rewarding baking can be. I discovered that when I'm baking, I get really calm, and I lose track of time—in a good way. My mind has always felt like a hyper puppy, but not anymore. Not when I bake. I guess that's what it means to be in a flow state. I can't believe how much I enjoy creating something that looks beautiful and tastes delicious—something I hope will make other people happy.

I'm so grateful for the Porters, because they reintroduced me to something I'd forgotten how much I loved.

Marisa sniffled. Jack turned to her and mouthed *Thank you.*

Once I decided to make baking my hobby, I rode my bike to the library, where my mom used to work. I hadn't been there since she got sick. I was just hoping to check out some cookbooks for beginners, but I ended up not wanting to leave. It's very peaceful there, surrounded by books, whistle chairs, and my mom's best friend. If I hadn't started baking, I'm not sure I ever would've gone back, and that would've been terrible.

Now Norm sniffled. Jack reached over and squeezed his arm.

I want to be on the next season of The Marvelous Midwest Kids Baking Championship *so bad. I want to show the world that anybody can bake, even a boy from the Northwoods who might not look like a typical baker.*

If you choose me for the next season of MMKBC, I know I won't be the best one on the show, because there's still a lot for me to learn. But I'll be able to inspire other kids. I can prove to them that anything is possible, thanks to practice, persistence, and good friends. They're the most important ingredients you'll ever need.

In summary, I hope you'll invite me to Chicago to audition. I'm thirteen years old, so this is my only chance to try out. Thank you for your time, and please give a big hello to Shane, Vicky, and Archie for me.

Jack had filmed his audition video in such a hurry, he barely remembered what he'd said. But now, he was relieved to find he wouldn't change a thing—except maybe the "give a big hello to Shane, Vicky, and Archie" part. Everything that had come out of his mouth had been right and true.

The video began to show the photographs that Jack had taken of his Presidential Pride, and there was a voiceover from Shane O'Shaughnessy:

> *Jack has named his sheet cake Presidential Pride. Featuring undertones of vanilla, it celebrates the flavor of pure, organic almond extract, and the frosting serves as a perfect neutral base for his patriotic mosaic of sprinkles.*

"That cake was *good*," Norm whispered.
"You ate half of it," Jack whispered back, cheerfully.
Shane O'Shaughnessy went on:

> *Thanks to his mother, an American history buff, Jack was named after three presidents. He knows from reading extensively about Andrew Jackson, Thomas Jefferson, and Woodrow Wilson that*

they were rather unusual. Interesting, flawed, and headstrong, they accomplished great things. They made mistakes, too—some big, some small. Like all of us, they were human.

Jack says, "I made my Presidential Pride to show the world that I can aim high and soar, just like the meteor on my cake. It might take me a while, but I'm going to find my way."

The lights went on, and the screen went up.

Jack stood a little straighter. He'd been right. His journey had been twisty, but he'd gotten exactly where he'd needed to go.

Norm nudged him. "How'd they know all that stuff about you?"

"I had to answer questions—a *lot* of questions." Jack grinned.

"Are you ready?" Betsy said.

"Ready as I'll ever be." Jack stepped toward Betsy, and there was a chorus of *Good luck, buddy! Good luck, Prez! Good luck, Jackers!*

He imagined his mom joining in, too. *Good luck, Jellybean! I love you!*

"I'll be here waiting," Norm called out from behind. "I won't leave until you're done."

Jack turned around, and they locked eyes. "Thanks, Dad."

"Knock their socks off, buddy."

"I will." Jack had never been so sure of anything before.

And then he took a deep breath and strode toward the sound of Shane O'Shaughnessy's voice and the life-changing smell of butter, cinnamon, and sugar.

Acknowledgements

Writing a book and sending it out into the world is an unbelievably nerve-wracking and joyful endeavor. I'm fortunate to do it a second time only because of the support I've received from my family: Chip, Owen, Caroline, Jane, the Original Six (Dan, Cindy, Elizabeth, Emily, and Anne, along with their spouses and my sweet niblings), Aunt Susy, and all the Merritts and Birds.

Special thanks to Em for a precious boost of encouragement when I needed it most, and to my cousin Jeff for unintentionally giving me the idea for Norm's nuggies.

I greatly appreciate the tireless librarians, teachers, indie bookshop owners, reporters, and students who have invited me to speak about my book and the power of middle grade fiction. I'm thrilled to do it all over again with *Marvelous Jackson*.

Mary Kole at Good Story Company is a brilliant and exacting editor who has pushed me, draft after maddening draft, to write clearer and better. I owe her a debt of gratitude.

The team at Orange Hat Publishing is top-notch. Thanks especially to Shannon Ishizaki, Michael Braun, Lauren Blue, Jayden Ellsworth, Elliott Haberer, Addison Haberer, and Kaeley Dunteman-Stiefvater for going above and beyond.

I applaud the Independent Book Publishers Association, the Midwest Independent Publishers Association, and the Arts + Literature Laboratory for promoting literature, and for recognizing my first novel in such meaningful ways.

Thank you to Thomson Weir, LLC for my crash course in publicity and messaging. I would be a bumbling fool without Mike and his knowledgeable, gracious team.

I am beyond fortunate to have dear friends near and far—including those in the fabulous Bookstagram community—who have reviewed my books, invited me to their book groups, posted beautiful things on social media, and sent me reassuring messages. I love you all.

Marvelous Jackson

A huge shout-out goes to Gooch's A-One Bar & Grill in Boulder Junction, which has the best broasted chicken in Wisconsin and was my inspiration for Dutch's.

Finally, I wrote this book for all the Jacksons out there, along with the loving people who help them get where they want to go. This kind of support is sweeter than any dessert.

**Have you read *Crossing the Pressure Line*?
It's where Jack's story begins.**

Full of heart and inspiration, *Crossing the Pressure Line* is the perfect book for kids who love swimming, fishing, animals, and the outdoors. It's about setting fierce goals and learning to listen to the courageous voice inside.

Happy reading!

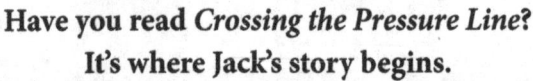

Bonus Content: MARVELOUS Recipes!

Whimsydiddles

Recipe by Jenny MacReady at MacReady Artisan Bread Company in Egg Harbor, WI

Ingredients:

1 cup (salted) brown butter (cooled but still liquid)
1½ cups brown sugar
2 eggs
2 tsp vanilla
2⅔ cups flour
2 tsp cream of tartar
1 tsp baking soda
2 tsp cinnamon
½ cup Rice Krispies

For rolling:
2 tbsp white sugar
2 tsp cinnamon

Directions:

Heat oven to 350 degrees.

Brown butter on the stovetop and set aside to cool. Measure all other ingredients and set aside. Mix melted butter, brown sugar, eggs, and vanilla thoroughly in the mixer using a paddle attachment. If no mixer is available, this can be done by hand in a large mixing bowl. In a separate bowl, mix the flour, cream of tartar, baking soda, and cinnamon. Carefully add the dry ingredient mixture into the wet ingredient mixture one cup at a time. Mix until all ingredients are well blended. Remove bowl from mixer. Fold Rice Krispies into batter with a wooden spoon or spatula. Scoop out batter with an ice cream scoop onto a baking sheet that is covered with parchment paper. Roll dough balls in cinnamon sugar mixture before baking.

Bake 12-15 minutes in oven.

Vanilla Blooms

Recipe by Annemarie Maitri at Bloom Bake Shop in Madison, WI

Cookie Ingredients:
- 1½ cups unsalted butter (room temperature)
- 1¾ cups sugar
- 5 cups all-purpose flour
- 2¼ tsp baking powder
- ¾ tsp salt
- 1 large egg, plus 1 yolk
- 1 tbsp vanilla
- ¼ cup whole milk

Confectionary Glaze Ingredients:
- 2 cups sifted powdered sugar
- 2-4 tbsp whole milk
- 1 tsp vanilla extract
- Shimmery sprinkles

Directions:

Gather and measure all your ingredients. Ensure butter is room temperature. Sift flour, baking powder, and salt into a bowl. Set aside.

Cream butter and sugar for about 3-5 minutes on medium speed until light and creamy. Add in eggs, one at a time, and mix until combined, careful not to overmix.

Mix vanilla and whole milk together in a separate bowl.

Alternate your dry ingredients with your milk and vanilla to the butter and sugar mixture, mixing and scraping down the sides and the bottom of the bowl in between additions.

Chill dough for 1 hour. Roll dough into walnut-sized balls and place 2 inches apart onto ungreased baking sheets. Bake at 350 degrees (conventional oven) for 12-15 minutes.

Cool before glazing.

Maple Blueberry Muffins

Recipe by Pam Murphy at Tilly's in Rhinelander, WI

Ingredients:
- 2 cups flour
- ¾ tsp baking soda
- ¾ tsp baking powder
- ½ tsp cinnamon
- ¾ tsp sea salt
- ¾ cup blueberries
- 8 tbsp unsalted butter, softened (1 stick)
- ½ cup maple syrup
- ¾ cup sour cream
- 3 tbsp light brown sugar
- 1 tsp vanilla
- 2 eggs
- 1½ cups confectioners' powdered sugar
- 2 tbsp maple syrup
- 1 tbsp cream

Directions:

Prepare a 12-muffin cupcake pan by placing a paper liner in each. Preheat the oven to 350 degrees.

Mix together flour, baking soda, baking powder, cinnamon, and salt in a bowl and set aside. Fold blueberries in the flour mixture, being careful not to smash. Beat butter, maple syrup, sour cream, brown sugar, and vanilla together, adding eggs one at a time, beating well after each. With a large spoon, fold the dry ingredients into the butter mixture, being careful not to smash the berries.

The muffin batter should be filled ¾ full. Place in the middle rack of a preheated oven.

Bake the muffins until puffed and golden and a toothpick inserted in the center comes out clean, approximately 15-20 minutes.

Let the muffins cool in the pan 5 minutes, then remove to a rack to finish cooling.

Maple Glaze Directions:

Whisk powdered sugar, maple syrup, and cream until smooth. Drizzle glaze over warm muffins with a spoon.